WORKFORCE EDUCATION FOR LATINOS

Politics, Programs, and Practices

ANA G. HUERTA-MACÍAS

Bergin & Garvey
Westport, Connecticut • London

Library of Congress Cataloging-in-Publication Data

Huerta-Macías, Ana.
    Workforce education for Latinos : politics, programs, and practices /
Ana G. Huerta-Macías.
        p.   cm.
    Includes bibliographical references and index.
    ISBN 0–89789–808–7 (alk. paper)
    1. Workplace literacy—United States.   2. Hispanic Americans—Education
(Continuing education)   3. Education, Bilingual—United States.   I. Title.
    LC149.7.H84   2002
    374.1829′68073—dc21   2001037912

British Library Cataloguing in Publication Data is available.

Library of Congress Catalog Card Number: 2001037912
ISBN: 0–89789–808–7

First published in 2002

Bergin & Garvey, 88 Post Road West, Westport, CT 06881
An imprint of Greenwood Publishing Group, Inc.
www.greenwood.com

Printed in the United States of America

The paper used in this book complies with the
Permanent Paper Standard issued by the National
Information Standards Organization (Z39.48–1984).

10 9 8 7 6 5 4 3 2 1

CONTENTS

A photo essay follows chapter 3.

‖ ILLUSTRATIONS

| PREFACE

The demographic landscape of the United States has changed dramatically over the last several decades. Linguistically and culturally diverse groups have greatly increased in numbers. Latinos constitute the largest of the ethnic groups and have received much attention from business and the media. Business, for example, has studied and projected the economic and cultural significance of this group for years and has targeted Latinos through Spanish-language advertising and products geared specifically to them, such as foods, music, magazines, and television programs. The influence of Latinos in the United States has been so great that *Time* magazine published a special issue on June 11, 2001, entitled "The border is vanishing before our eyes, creating a new world for all of us: Welcome to Amexica." It seems that educational institutions, however, are always lagging behind in coming to the realization that important societal developments are taking place that demand attention and a shift from outdated perspectives to new ones. High levels of bureaucratic inertia, at best, and xenophobia at worst, preclude change from taking place at a pace that keeps up with societal and cultural realities. Education for Latino adults is one such area.

Much of the current research literature has focused on curricular, instructional, and administrative issues that arise in working with Latino youth. Dual-language bilingual education programs, English-as-a-second-language curricula, culturally responsive pedagogy, and high-school dropout prevention constitute some of the areas of focus in the literature. Yet, most of this literature deals with preschool, elementary, middle, and

high-school students. Adult education as a field has received relatively little attention. Specifically, the education of Latino adults has received much
less attention, and attention to educational issues relevant to the Latino
workforce with low levels of literacy and schooling has received virtually
no attention at all. It is this latter group that is the focus of this research. It is
incumbent upon educators, administrators, and industry to focus on Latino and Latina students and workers, for the statistics indicate that we are
a very young population who will comprise the largest segment of the
workforce in the United States in the coming decades. This book is about
education for Latinos who are at the bottom of the educational and economic ladder, and who find themselves unemployed, displaced, and/or
looking for advancement. The picture for this segment of the Latino
workforce is currently a very bleak one in terms of the types of positions
that they occupy—low-wage, dead-end jobs that provide no opportunity
for advancement. The majority of this group has found itself in low-paying
agricultural, manufacturing, or service industry jobs that are the most
prone to layoffs, abolishment, and segregation from advancement opportunities. They have also been underserved by the adult education system in
the United States.

This lack of equitable access to education that is responsive to the needs
and interests of Latino and Latina workers is the same one that has plagued
public-school education for decades. Long-term education, as opposed to a
six-week course in specific job skills training, for instance, is the key to advancement. Yet, many Latinos are not receiving these opportunities, even
though they are the ones who have carried this country to the economic
prosperity it has enjoyed over the last few decades. Latino labor, for instance, has provided fresh fruits and vegetables, durable goods such as
jeans, computers, and television sets, and cleaning and other services at a
low cost to consumers in the United States. They have also borne the brunt
of recent legislation—including welfare reform and the North American
Free Trade Agreement (NAFTA)—that has impacted them negatively.
Again, little attention is being paid to remedying these political, economic,
and educational problems, which stem from misguided, myopic, and discriminatory policies of government, business, and educational entities.

This book illuminates some of these issues as relevant to federally subsidized workforce education programs. Chapter 1 provides an introduction
with some background information on workforce education and Latinos.
Chapter 2 discusses current legislation that has negatively impacted Latinos and fleshes out the issues by providing a close look at a Borderland city
in the southwest where the Latino workforce has suffered greatly from displacement and unemployment. Chapter 3 presents a description of educational programs that are successfully assisting Latino workers in their
search for advancement, and addresses the issue of language use in instruction for Latinos. Chapter 4 highlights some exemplary instructional prac-

tices. Chapter 5 discusses the issues of accountability and assessment in adult education, and chapter 6 lays out recommendations for changes in policies in workforce education for Latinos.

It is appropriate here to explain some of the terminology used in this book. The use of "Latino/a" vs. "Hispanic" is a perennial debate. Some argue that Hispanic is a colonistic term that has been imposed by the dominant society, while others feel that Latino is too liberal or radical. Some people use these terms interchangeably, depending on who is being addressed and what the individual preferences may be at the moment. The author uses "Latinos" in this book as an all-inclusive term to refer to Guatemalans, Salvadorans, Puerto-Ricans, Mexicans, Cubans, and all other Latin American subgroups. The term "Hispanic" is often used in the literature to mean the same thing. Thus, Hispanic is also used herein when discussing the research that has used this term—that is, the term used in a specific research study is preserved when reporting on that specific study or when reporting statistics. "Latino," unless specifically stated otherwise, includes both Latinos and Latinas. The author's intention is not to diminish the importance of Latinas in the workforce or the additional barriers that they face, such as gender discrimination. The intent, rather, is to provide a text that presents information and ideas as succinctly and accurately as possible. Thus, "Latino," the generic form of the word, is used.

"Workforce education" is also used as an inclusive term to include programs with two or more academic components—English as a second language, General Educational Development (GED), basic literacy in English and or Spanish, and so forth—as well as job-skills training in a selected occupation. The term "workforce education" as used by the author differs from "workforce development" or "workforce training" as used in some of the literature from the Department of Labor and other sources, in that the emphasis is on education rather than on job training. Education as used herein includes study that focuses on the development of conceptual knowledge and other cognitive and metacognitive skills that prepare a student for lifelong learning and continued education to the GED and beyond to a postsecondary credential (such as a license in an occupation, an associate two-year degree, or a four-year degree). Education may also include job-skills training as part of the curriculum for lifelong learning. However, the emphasis is on providing a foundation for continued learning at the postsecondary level. Workforce "training," on the other hand, focuses on short-term rather than long-term needs and emphasizes skill development and job placement in a given occupation. The author has used the term "workforce education" in keeping with the goal of education as lifelong learning for positive change in any or all aspects of one's personal and professional life. This is opposed to quick-fix approaches that provide only enough skills to fill the first job that becomes available, with little or no support for the worker to continue his or her education to levels that permit entry into higher paying jobs with potential for advancement.

Through this book the author hopes to bring to the forefront issues and programs relative to adult education that are unique to Latinos and, specifically, to the Latino population in the U.S.–Mexico Borderlands. The Borderlands often receive negative attention, as the media often portray this region as one filled with crime, drugs, poverty, and other problems (issues that are, in effect, rooted in political and social inequities created by those in power although not recognized as such). In reality, the Borderlands is a region that is providing the country not only with richness in terms of literature, music, and language, but also with innovative research and thinking dealing with global issues in education, economics, health, and other areas. This area is providing models for the rest of the country in terms of educational programs for Latinos at all levels—from preschoolers to adults, and from dual- and tri-language public-school education to integrated models of bilingual workforce education for adults. It is worthwhile, then, to view the educational advances in the Borderlands as a model for an increasingly diverse and global world.

Last, I wish to thank all of those who, knowingly and unknowingly, contributed to this book. The many dialogues I have had with colleagues at all levels and the places and classes that have opened their doors to me during my visits have enriched my perspectives and helped make the writing of this book possible. I am also indebted to those individuals who reviewed earlier versions of the chapters in this book and provided insightful comments and suggestions.

I am particularly grateful to all of those workers who inspired this research as they continue to strive for a better education and livelihood, and as they so poignantly present their case to educators, researchers, administrators, and legislators. It is the purpose of the book to make their stories known to many others and to effect a change in thinking and policy. Finally, I wish to thank my own family—Carmen Gabriela, Jose Andrés, and Francisco Federico—who have each, in unique ways, contributed to and encouraged my scholarship, and thank my extended family, the Huertas, all of whom have been an inspiration to me in terms of their constant search for education and excellence.

ABBREVIATIONS

ABE	Adult Basic Education
ACT	American College Testing
AEA	Adult Education Act
AFDC	Aid to Families with Dependent Children
BEST	Basic English Skills Test
BVT	Bilingual Vocational Training
CASAS	Comprehensive Adult Student Assessment System
CET	Center for Employment Training
EFF	Equipped for the Future
ESL	English as a Second Language
GAO	General Accounting Office
GED	General Educational Development
GPRA	Government Performance and Review Act (of 1993)
JOBS	Job Opportunities and Basic Skills
JTPA	Job Training Partnership Act
NAFTA	North American Free Trade Agreement
NALS	National Adult Literacy Survey
NCA	New Concurrent Approach
NEA	National Education Act

NIFL   National Institute for Literacy
NLRA   National Labor Relations Act
NRS   National Reporting System
NSSB   National Skills Standard Board
NWLP   National Workplace Literacy Program
PREP   Proactive Re-Employment Project
PRWORA   Personal Responsibility and Work Opportunity Reconcilia-
            tion Act
SCANS   Secretary's Commission for Achieving Necessary Skills
TAA   Trade Adjustment Assistance
TABE   Test of Adult Basic English
TANF   Temporary Assistance to Needy Families
TESOL   Teaching English to Speakers of Other Languages
TWC   Texas Workforce Commission
VESL   Vocational English as a Second Language
WARN   Worker Adjustment and Retraining Notification
WIA   Workforce Investment Act
WLPB   Woodcock Language Proficiency Battery
WtW   Welfare-to-Work

1

THE LANDSCAPE OF LATINOS, EDUCATION, AND WORK

Latinos are the largest ethnic group in the country. According to the U.S. Census Bureau there are now 35.3 million Latinos, representing about 13 percent of the U.S. population. This group, moreover, is growing 53 percent faster than the total U.S. population. By the year 2050, it is estimated that Latinos will number 87.4 million, accounting for 25 percent of the population (Brooke, 2000).

The Spanish language is part of the cultural heritage of this group and is the one common bond among the Cuban, Puerto Rican, Mexican, Salvadoran, Guatemalan, and other Latino groups. It is estimated that Spanish is the first language of approximately 93 percent of U.S. Latinos, now making the United States the fifth-largest Spanish-speaking country after Mexico, Spain, Argentina, and Colombia. Some researchers estimate that by 2010, it will be the second largest, after Mexico (Brooke, 2000). Additionally, while the majority population is aging, Latinos in the United States are a very young group. The latest U.S. Census figures indicate that 35 percent of Hispanics are under age eighteen, as compared to 25.7 percent of the U.S. population. The median age for Hispanics is 25.9 years while that of the entire U.S. population is 35.3 years (U.S. Census Bureaus, 2001).

Latinos as an ethnic group are receiving more attention because of their numbers and their potential power. Business, for instance, began marketing products specifically for Latinos several years ago, and advertising in Spanish is now quite prevalent. Telephone call centers around the country have hired Spanish speakers for their telemarketing, and both Al Gore and George W. Bush, contenders in the presidential race of 2000, were working very hard to lure the Latino vote. However, the political and educational system as a whole continues to fail Latinos. More than 30 percent of Latino children, for instance, live in poverty, the highest rate ever. California (holding 34% of the Latino population in the U.S.) has passed propositions limiting immigrant rights, and 66 percent of Hispanics (compared to 41 percent of non-Hispanic whites) have little or no college education (Larmer, 1999).

Educators in the United States have been conducting research studies on Latinos for at least four decades. Early studies in the area of bilingual education, for instance, focused on the Spanish-speaking students enrolled in the Coral Way Elementary School in Dade County in southern Florida in the sixties. The Bilingual Education Act was introduced in 1967 with the purpose of helping native speakers of Spanish who were failing in the school system (Baker, 1996). The educational research literature focusing on the educational achievement of Latinos has proliferated since then. Areas of emphasis are bilingual education (American Educational Research Association, 1992; Faltis and Hudelson, 1998), best practices (González, Huerta-Macías, and Tinajero, 1998; Hayes, Bahruth, and Kessler, 1991), high-school dropouts (Lockwood, 1996; Romo and Falbo, 1996), early-childhood rearing practices (Valdés, 1996), literature and culture (Heyck, 1994), and politics and identity (Donato, 1999; Oboler, 1995).

Relatively little attention, however, has been paid to Latinos as a group in adult education. Most of the literature in this area focuses on immigrants and English language learning in general (Benesch, 1991; Weinstein-Shr and Quintero, 1995), or on the nontraditional, older student returning to school (Merriam and Caffarella, 1999; Quigley, 1997). The National Institute for Literacy recently issued a policy statement based on the National Literacy Summit 2000, in which they recognized that over 50 percent of adult students today are English-language learners. However, they did not even acknowledge that Latinos constitute by far the largest group of adult English-as-a-Second-Language (ESL) students, much less make recommendations pertinent to them as the most numerous ethnic group (National Institute for Literacy, 2000c).

ADULT EDUCATION: CURRENT ISSUES

Adult education and literacy programs have received relatively little attention compared to public-school education. As will be discussed in chapter 2, federal initiatives for adult education were virtually nonexistent until the 1980s. These initiatives were fueled by reports on the part of educators, employers, and policy-makers that our youth were ill prepared to take on the new, high-tech jobs of the twenty-first century. In addition, a wave of publicity by the media on the high rate of illiteracy in the nation arose in the eighties that was designed to involve more people, either as volunteers or as learners, in adult literacy programs. Over the last two decades, adult education programs have evolved that provide ESL, vocational education, General Educational Development (GED), citizenship classes, and other types of instruction. The term Adult Basic Education (ABE) is used to refer to those programs subsidized by state and/or federal monies that include basic levels of reading, writing, and mathematics (often referred to as "numeracy"). GED is considered to be at the high level of adult education programs. There is a range of other programs funded by government agencies, educational institutions, business, and/or community-based organizations, which are offered to adults. These include, for instance, basic literacy programs that teach adults how to read and write, personal development classes, and parenting programs.

The discourse on adult education currently involves issues relating to retention, the professionalization of instructors, accountability, curriculum, and instruction. Retention in programs is a major concern for program administrators and adult educators. One report estimated that the 1979 dropout rate from various ABE and literacy programs was as high as 80 percent. Another study that looked at data from a twelve-month period in 1993–1994 indicated that the overall attrition rate in basic literacy in GED classes that were federally funded was 74 percent. These studies also indicated that those students who drop out tend to be in the low-literacy category (Quigley, 1997). D'Amico (1997) writes that "median retention rates across adult education programs are less than 60 hours per learner" (p. 6). While issues such as transportation, money, and child care often cause learners to drop out, the literature has suggested that there are additional issues that have yet to be investigated. One of these has to do with the false assumption that all learners share a common background and will therefore be responsive to a singular type of traditional instruction—an issue that has been extensively discussed in regard to public-school education (Cummins, 1989; González, Huerta-Macías, Tinajero, 1998; Olsen, 1997) but not to adult education. The research literature on public-school students, moreover, has confirmed that traditional types of curricula and instruction serve mainstream students but exclude Latinos and other minority students (Lucas, 1997; Olsen, 1997), a situation that is paralleled in adult education.

Professionalization of the adult-education teaching force is another issue that has received widespread attention, particularly within the last decade. Many adult education and literacy instructors have very limited training. In the case of ESL, many are hired on the basis of having had some college work and speaking English. Additionally, there is little attention paid to professional development once personnel are hired. The majority of these instructors are employed on a part-time basis, thus making it even more difficult to require any type of sustained professional training for them. Quigley (1997) reports that a study on federally funded programs in adult literacy found that over 80 percent of the staff worked part-time, and only 31 percent of the teaching force reported having any qualifications to teach adults. Beder (cited in Quigley, 1997) reported that, unlike the public-school system where all teachers are expected to have certification, in 1989 only "eleven states required certification in adult literacy. . . . Fourteen states required certification in elementary/secondary, but not adult education. Twenty-five states required no certification" (p. 9). Foster (1990) writes that the major problem in the professionalization of the adult education instructors is the missing infrastructure. "Literacy programs are a bastard of the educational system—isolated from the mainstream and deprived of adequate resources for health, growth, and development" (p. 81). Shanahan, Mehan, and Mogge (1995) add that teacher preparation requirements and funding are reciprocal. "States with teacher preparation requirements contribute a much greater share of their total adult basic education allocation to teacher preparation than do states with no such requirements, which suggests that the professionalization of teachers is part of a comprehensive commitment to adult literacy education in these states" (p. 1). Some of the solutions to the lack of professionalization are (1) increased funding that will enable programs to conduct professional development activities and compensate the instructors for participation in these activities, and (2) an agreement on teacher preparation requirements.

The lack of standards for accountability is a related issue that has plagued adult education. Typically, programs will define their own accountability measures by their individual goals and objectives and use diverse sources of data to identify the outcomes. These include, for instance, portfolios with student work samples, standardized test results, attendance records, and/or attainment of credentials such as the GED or U.S. citizenship. However, there is often a mismatch between what program administrators consider adequate indicators of performance and what funding agencies consider to be adequate. For example, whereas funding entities often call for the use of standardized tests, many educators prefer to use alternative assessment measures. The lack of funding stems, to some extent, from the fact that there have been no standards that have been applied across programs. Therefore, it becomes difficult to identify the characteristics of those programs that are successful and that merit funding.

The unavailability of appropriate measures that can document success among programs that service linguistically and culturally diverse students is another problem. As D'Amico (1997) states, "Many of the achieved outcomes of adult education go unrecorded because we lack appropriate measures for capturing such outcomes, or because more expensive qualitative and longitudinal studies are needed to understand the varied impacts of adult education over time" (p. 6). At the heart of the matter is the fact that the purpose of literacy varies across programs. In some programs, specific work-related skills are the goal, while in others it is social change or attainment of specific credentials, such as the GED. The quality of instruction also varies greatly across programs. Thus, as Merrifield (1998) stated: "Adult basic education is struggling to create a national accountability system without a national service delivery system" (p. 2). Equipped for the Future (EFF), a project of the National Institute for Literacy, has developed a framework with four purposes for adult education and lifelong learning that is expected to fill the void for a curricular and assessment framework. EFF focuses on what adults need to know and be able to do in their roles as workers; parents and family members, and citizens and community members.

This framework, developed by the National Institute for Literacy, is expected to have a great impact on all of adult education because it provides a set of standards and skills around which quality curricula may be developed and learners may be assessed. EFF standards support the accountability requirements defined by recent legislation, and will have an increasing impact on workforce education as providers become more proficient in the framework and assessment measures are developed to accompany the framework. Standards for adult education ESL programs have been recently developed by Teaching English to Speakers of Other Languages (TESOL), the foremost professional organization in the field. These standards address (1) program structure, administration, and planning, (2) curriculum, (3) instruction, and (4) recruitment, intake, and orientation (TESOL Task Force, 2000). Benchmarks are provided for each area that serve as indicators of program quality. Current legislation in welfare reform has recently called for a comprehensive accountability system of performance that meets certain defined criteria. It is expected that adult education programs will increasingly look to EFF as they grapple with the development of systems that meet the federal requirements, and that those programs serving Latinos and other linguistically and culturally diverse groups will also integrate the TESOL standards into their programs.

Curriculum and instruction that are appropriate for the diversity of the adult population are additional challenges in the field of adult education. The content to be taught for specific credentials that require a passing score on standardized examinations (such as the GED or commercial driver license) has already been identified. However, deciding what is to be taught to learners in basic literacy, ESL, or ABE classes is more difficult. Recent federal legislation in welfare reform has greatly tightened governmental authority over education and essentially presented a situation to adult educators and administrators in which they either orient their teaching toward the development of skills for employment or lose federal funding. Consequently, many educators who believe in the broader purposes of education (such as personal empowerment, advocacy, and challenging of inequitable conditions) are facing ideological dilemmas.

Compounding this issue are the interests and goals of adult learners, who want to be able to compete in the global economy as workers but who also want to go beyond the world of the workplace and exercise their roles successfully as family and community members and as citizens (Stein,

1997). During the early federal initiatives in the eighties, the emphasis was on increasing the number of adult education and literacy programs. The quality of the programs in existence or of new programs that were emerging was not addressed (Soifer et al., 1990). The implementation of appropriate methods of instruction that will meet the needs and interests of learners is a challenge that has still not been met by adult education. Many classes are still taught using traditional and mainstream methods of instruction, where the activities focus on repetition and fill-in-the-blanks workbook exercises. Most instructors are not trained in the current interactive instructional methods that are based on generative dialogue, learner construction of knowledge, project implementation, and the infusion of technology as a tool to enhance learning. Purcell-Gates, Degener, and Jacobson (1998) reported, for example, that of 271 adult literacy programs in the United States that they studied, "73 percent can be described as using activities and materials that are not related to their students' lives and are teacher directed and controlled rather than collaborative" (p. 1). These issues of retention, professionalization, accountability, curriculum, and instruction, which the current discourse on adult education comprises, have become particularly acute in the area of workforce education.

WORKFORCE EDUCATION

Adult education as it occurs in formal learning settings (as opposed to informal learning opportunities that occur throughout our lives) includes workplace literacy (consisting of literacy development classes at the work site), vocational education (training for job-specific credentials—such as those required for becoming an electrician or machinist); and workforce education (including not only job-specific skills but also broader academic skills). Literacy development, whether in the first and/or second language, is foundational to all of these programs. Thus, the terms "adult education" and "adult literacy" are often used interchangeably. Adult-education programs integrate literacy development and, similarly, literacy programs often include content from basic education programs as the vehicle for literacy development.

Workplace literacy programs were generated by the need on the part of industry for competent workers who possessed those skills necessary for success at the work site. These programs traditionally focused on developing curricula for specific vocational areas using what is called "task analysis." This involves the instructor or appropriate individual going into a workplace, observing and interviewing workers, and analyzing the performance requirements of the jobs in question in order to create a list of "skills requirements," which are then taught to the program participants. While this approach undeniably made learning more concrete, it in essence replaced one form of literacy—school literacy—with another, work literacy.

The concern that developed on the part of educators was that, rather than broadening the array of literacy skills of the students (i.e., to include not only work-related practices but also literature, citizenship, communication in diverse settings, using technology for problem solving, etc.), the workplace curriculum narrowed literacy to work practices as defined by lists of skills generated by job audits or task analyses. Using work to drive content and examples made it difficult to implement more student-centered approaches.

Another concern over this work-applied curriculum was that it often led to more traditional, skill-and-drill-type pedagogy as opposed to the more current pedagogies, which utilize dialogue, cooperative learning, projects, and other such activities consistent with the new emphasis on education for critical thinking and empowerment. In the recent past, employers have also become concerned as they increasingly realize that the skills they are demanding of their workers have changed significantly from those called for two decades ago, when many workplace literacy programs were initiated.

Baba's (1991) research on an anthropological description of diverse work activities provides examples of the changing workplace and the need for more than job-specific skills. These descriptions include, for instance, an automobile plant where workers collaboratively problem-solve and plan in advance of their work day in order to meet objectives; craftsmen who negotiate with each other, analyze the economics of the extra time required on the job to produce twice as much, dialogue, and come to an agreement on ways to increase productivity; and copier technicians who problem-solve orally as they discuss information and diagnosis involved in copier repair and mentally store information, which they later retrieve as needed. Darrah (1997) added to this body of research literature with a study that explained how the workers at a computer-assembly plant were expected to (1) do descriptive and prescriptive writing; (2) understand the entire manufacturing process in order to accurately perform the calculations needed to order parts; (3) foresee problems such as delays in obtaining necessary parts and delays due to absenteeism among team members, and (4) determine a daily production target.

Employers now want employees to work "smarter" and not "harder." Thus, the following skills are mentioned frequently by employers as desirable for employees at all levels: "Knowing how to learn; competence in reading, writing, and computation; effective listening and oral communication skills; adaptability through creative thinking and problem solving; personal management with strong self-esteem and initiative; interpersonal skills; the ability to work in teams or groups; leadership effectiveness; and basic technology skills" (Imel, 1999, pp. 1–2). However, there is a contradiction that still exists regarding what employers want. As Grubb (1996) states, "On the one hand, employers value highly job specific skills.... They often criticize educational institutions for including too much 'theory' and general education. . . . Yet, employees also complain about the lack of general and 'academic' capacities, including the ability to read, write, and communicate in other ways" (p. 28). What the real issue may be, he explains, is that the skills required at entry level are much more specific than those required for job advancement and increasing responsibility. "The problem for students and educational providers is that the skills necessary in the *short* run may obscure the skills necessary for promotion and mobility in the *long* run" (p. 29). Nonetheless, workforce education programs have evolved as distinct from workplace literacy programs because they include these broader, more academic-type skills—although to differing degrees, depending on the specific program.

The emphasis on increased communication skills in English for many jobs has made it particularly difficult for Spanish-dominant or Spanish-monolingual Latinos to obtain employment and benefit from traditional workforce-education programs that are taught in English. ESL instruction provided by employers or by educational institutions has been the solution to these problems. The curricula for this instruction are derived from the work activities of the participants: "language structures, functions, and vocabulary are drawn from the work life of the participants and can range from discrete study of specialized vocabulary items, to the more abstract and often convoluted language used in procedures manuals or benefits packets, to the language needed to communicate with co-workers" (McGroarty and Scott, 1993, p. 1).

Unions have also sponsored ESL instruction for the workplace. Unlike workplace instructional programs, union-sponsored ESL has included not only competency-based job skills but also general life skills and worker-centered education. These curricula, for example, include workplace rights, safety, and health instruction, the rationale being that immigrant workers tend to hold the more hazardous, lower paying jobs and are often exploited by employers because they cannot advocate for themselves. Another reason for the emphasis on workplace rights, safety, and health is that Spanish-speaking workers are reported to suffer job injuries 80 percent more often than other workers (Rosenblum, 1996). However, despite ESL class offerings from employers, unions, educational institutions, and community-based organizations, the demand for adult ESL instruction far exceeds the availability of classes, so that there are thousands of people on waiting lists for ESL classes around the country (Waggoner, 1997). Additionally, there are many who are interested in classes but do not enroll because they face barriers of time, money, childcare, and transportation (National Center for Education Statistics, 1998).

The issue of Latinos' lack of access to education begins in the public schools, which have also been unresponsive to their needs. Latinos drop out of high school more often than any other group, including blacks (White House Initiative on Educational Excellence for Hispanic Americans, 1999). Because a high-school diploma is the credential that is expected for just about every mid-level (technicians, clerks, electricians, etc.) subbaccalaureate job (Grubb, 1996), it is logical that Latinos suffer high rates of unemployment and/or very low-paying jobs with nonsustainable wages.

The National Center for Education Statistics (1999b) indicates that 27.1 percent of Hispanic high-school dropouts were unemployed in 1998. The unemployment rate for Latinos has become particularly acute in the U.S.–Mexico Borderlands, where the North American Free Trade Agreement (NAFTA) has added another major dimension to the complexity of the workforce education scenario (see chapter 3). The opportunities for workforce education appear quite dismal for Latinos, given the population statistics described above, the high drop-out rate for Hispanics, and the limited availability and support for ESL instruction and workforce education.

A recent report by the National Council of La Raza confirms that great numbers of Latinos are stagnating in low-wage jobs. A very disturbing finding is that since 1980, the proportion of Latinos in agriculture, retail trade, and service industries is increasing even though these are among the lowest paid jobs. The explanation is that the low educational and skill levels of Latinos do not allow access to better paying jobs. Additionally, Latino men have been found to have the highest participation rate in the labor force. That is, they are—among white and all ethnic groups—the males most likely to be working or looking for a job (Siles and Perez, 2000). Currently, one in 10 workers is Latino, even though Latinos are far less likely than other minorities or Anglos to fill management positions (Chapa and Wacker, 2000). They are concentrated in low-wage jobs, with little opportunity to get the education that could lead to job advancement. Another often overlooked factor that has kept Latinos in low-wage jobs is employment discrimination. Research has shown that discrimination has occurred during the recruitment and hiring processes, through tracking or segregation on the job, and through lack of mentoring and representation in decision-making positions (Melendez, cited in Morales, 2000).

The increased globalization and restructuring of industry has also had a negative impact on Latinos. The many job losses in manufacturing jobs, which have high concentrations of Latinos, has increased inequality in income. Morales (2000) writes, "By 1997, Latinos became the poorest racial/ethnic group in the country. . . . That year, Latinos constituted nearly one quarter (24 percent) of the nation's poor" (p. 59). The claim has been made that the influx of immigration from Central and South America accounts for this poverty. However, in 1990, the average poverty rate for Hispanic immigrants was only 0.7 percentage points higher than for native-born Hispanics. Therefore, the high Latino poverty rate in the United States can hardly be attributed to immigrants, as is claimed by some policymakers. Despite this bleak picture, education and skills development, the keys to moving up the economic ladder, remain inaccessible to the majority of Latino workers. Federal initiatives, moreover, have hindered rather than increased the Latino workforce's access to education.

2

THE POLITICS OF WORKFORCE EDUCATION

Legislation in adult education has determined the design of programs that are developed, including the content of the curriculum, the types of students that are served, the length of the program, and the types of support services that are offered to the participants. A historical perspective of legislation in adult education provides an understanding of how the politics inherent in this legislation has affected adult education.

ADULT EDUCATION: A LEGISLATIVE HISTORY

The Adult Education Act (AEA), enacted in 1966, was the only federal commitment to adult literacy prior to the early eighties. This legislation provided grants to states for the improvement of adult literacy. However, there was little interest in this Act, which was severely underfunded and treated learning as an end in itself. Interest in adult literacy was spurred to a large extent by the publication of *A Nation at Risk* in 1983, which warned that the nation's students were graduating from our nation's public schools ill-prepared to lead the lives of a productive and responsible citizenry. This was accompanied by a shift in the workplace from manufacturing to service and high-tech jobs, which required an increase in literacy and problem-solving skills. The result of this was a "job-skills gap"—a mismatch between job demands and the skills of the labor force. Chisman and Campbell (1990) pinpointed this problem by stating that "entry-level jobs in manufacturing are dwindling, but even in that sector, statistical process control and machines that require sophisticated electronic as opposed to mechanical repair are making math, not muscle, a prime job requirement" (p. 144). These developments led to a renewed concern over adult education from the perspective of job-related skills.

The Job Training Partnership Act (JTPA), under the Department of Labor, became effective in 1983 and was one of the first pieces of legislation that explicitly linked adult education to employment. This act coordinated state and local governments with the business community for effective program administration. Its purpose was to provide job-training services for economically disadvantaged adults and youth, dislocated workers, and others who faced barriers in finding employment (U.S. Department of Labor, 2000). In 1989, the JTPA was amended in such a way that the commitment to basic and applied skills was strengthened, with the ultimate goal of increasing employability, a trend that was reinforced in subsequent legislation (Chisman, 1990). This was followed by the Job Opportunities and Basic Skills (JOBS) Training Program, which was established by the Department of Health and Human Services in 1988 as part of the Family Support Act. The goal of this program was to enhance the employability of welfare recipients by providing them with basic literacy services and job placement assistance. This legislation also added the JOBS program as an education and training component to Aid to Families with Dependent Children (AFDC). The AFDC/JOBS programs provided support through welfare payments for individuals who were unable to find work or whose income fell below a certain level. AFDC payments could continue for an unlimited amount of time, and there were few work requirements attached.

In 1988 the AEA was reauthorized and injected with new programs that specifically stated the purpose of literacy to be improving employment skills and assisting individuals with limited English proficiency to integrate into society (Chisman, 1990). The National Workplace Literacy Program (NWLP) was one of the programs authorized under Section 371 of the Adult Education Act at this time. The goal of this program was to upgrade the literacy and basic skills training of the workforce for the purpose of improving job performance. Services under the NWLP could include adult basic education, adult secondary education, ESL classes, upgrading of skills to meet changes in workplace requirements, and support services such as transportation and childcare (U.S. Department of Education, 1998). The NWLP was not reauthorized for funding in 1996. Yet, it was unique among federal programs in having had a fairly strong record of serving Hispanics. A study during its first year of implementation found that 24 percent of those served were Hispanics, 20 percent were black, and 9 percent were of Asian descent. Additionally, 22 percent of the programs in the first three grant cycles exclusively served workers with limited English proficiency (Gillespie, 1996). Still, the program was not refunded after 1995.

Part of the U.S. Department of Education's new interest in providing leadership to look at adult education and literacy as ways to improve employability called for a connection between skills taught in the schools to the newly defined skills required for the changing workplace. The reasoning was that since the changing economy required more than the traditional basic skills of workers, new approaches to teaching in the schools were also required. The Secretary's Commission on Achieving Necessary Skills (SCANS) Report issued in 1991 identified five broad categories of competencies that would lead to a successful transition from school to work. These categories and their respective skills were as follows:

- Resources—identifies, organizes, plans and allocates resources
- Interpersonal—works with others on teams, teaches others, serves clients, exercises leadership, negotiates, and works with diversity
- Information—acquires, organizes, interprets, evaluates, and communicates information
- Systems—understands complex interrelationships and can distinguish trends, predict impacts, and monitor and correct performance
- Technology—works with a variety of technologies and can choose appropriate tools for the task (Lankard, 1995)

The SCANS report also called for revising the abstract approach to learning by using a cognitive apprenticeship model whereby the student-as-apprentice-learner would learn academic competencies in a meaningful context. The SCANS competencies have been widely used as a framework for curriculum development in tech-prep, school-to-work, and transitional workforce education programs.

Another impetus toward adult education and literacy came in 1993 when the results of the National Adult Literacy Survey (NALS) were published, the most comprehensive effort to date to evaluate the literacy levels of the U.S. population. The adults interviewed for this survey were asked to perform tasks that tested prose literacy (the ability to read), document literacy (the ability to find and use information in various types of materials) and quantitative literacy (using numbers embedded in print material to perform arithmetic operations). The results were reported using five levels of proficiencies, with level 1 being the lowest and level 5 displaying the highest literacy proficiencies. The NALS reported that nearly half of all adult Americans had scored in the lowest two levels of literacy. This meant that they could not, for example, write a brief letter explaining a billing error, enter information into an automobile-maintenance record form, or calculate the difference between the regular and sale prices of an item in an advertisement. Only 18 to 21 percent of participants scored in levels 4 and 5, while approximately 30 percent scored in level 3 (Barton, 1999; National Center on Adult Literacy, 1995; Quigley, 1997). This survey confirmed that we were far from meeting the National Education Goals for the year 2000, as set forth by the Bush administration, which specified in part that Americans would "possess the knowledge and skills necessary to compete in a global economy and exercise the rights and responsibilities of citizenship" (U.S. Department of Education, 2000a).

The developments described above set the stage for the current reform in adult education. Over the last two decades, the federal role in adult education and literacy has gone from almost no interest to an awakening that a great many adults in the United States have not been served well by the public school system and are ill prepared to take on the demands of twenty-first century society. Concomitantly, a variety of programs have evolved over the years, from those that focus on basic education, ESL literacy, and academic skills to those that have job training and placement as their main goals. The trend has been to replace programs that prepare students for lifelong learning with those with the more narrow focus of job preparation. The new emphasis is on work first.

CURRENT LEGISLATION: A FOCUS ON EMPLOYMENT

The latter part of the Clinton administration brought dramatic changes in welfare reform. Specifically, the Personal Responsibility and Work Opportunity Reconciliation Act (PRWORA) was passed in 1996 and replaced AFDC and JOBS, which were in place before PRWORA. The PRWORA provides block grants to each state and allows much flexibility with respect to how the new legislation is implemented. Temporary Assistance to Needy Families (TANF), for welfare participants, is included under the act. There are, however, two major changes in this welfare reform from what was in place previously. The first is that it stipulates a lifetime maximum of five years of welfare benefits. The second is that it also requires welfare recipients to work or participate in a defined work activity within twenty-four months of receiving benefits (Jenkins, 1999). Additionally, in order to receive full TANF funding, states must place a certain percentage of welfare participants into jobs or into a work activity as defined by the state (for example, job search, vocational education, or community service), and individuals must work a prescribed number of hours each week. The required percentage of individuals working and the number of hours worked each week increases from 20 hours a week and 25 percent of the participants working in 1997 to 30 hours of work a week and 50 percent of the participants working by the year 2002 (Knell, 1998).

The significance of this legislation is that it presents what has been labeled a Work First approach that requires welfare participants to search for and find a job before they engage in long-term education or training. This Work First approach was based on data that clearly linked poverty to low literacy skills. The data revealed, for example, that welfare recipients aged

17 to 21 read, on average, at the sixth-grade level; and that 50 percent of adults on welfare do not have a high-school diploma or GED. The outcome is that 43 percent of adults with low literacy skills live in poverty and 17 percent receive food stamps. Among adults with strong literacy skills, however, fewer than 5 percent live in poverty and less than 1 percent receive food stamps (National Institute for Literacy, 2000b) This legislation was, therefore, a response to criticism that the government was creating welfare dependency as well as supporting and even encouraging individuals to bypass any efforts towards creating self-sufficiency. The ultimate intent was to save federal dollars.

The Welfare-to-Work (WtW) Program of 1997 was one of the first additions to PRWORA and is administered by the Department of Labor. This act provides funds to states that are targeted toward those that are the least ready for jobs—that is, those with the lowest skills, who have been categorized as the "hardest-to-serve." At least 70 percent of WtW funds must be used to service TANF recipients who have received assistance for more than 30 months and/or are within 12 months of reaching their 60 month limit. The act provides funds for activities such as job placement and postemployment services. However, "stand-alone" activities, such as ESL instruction, are not eligible activities until a participant has begun working. The intent of WtW was to provide additional resources for the most disadvantaged welfare recipients, who would need extra services to succeed in their transition to work. Even though enrollments in this program have been increasing recently, WtW has not been as successful as expected because the legislative mandates and administrative structure attached to it have made it difficult for programs to identify and verify eligible participants (Nightingale and Trutko, 1999).

The Workforce Investment Act of 1998 replaced the Adult Education Act and the JOBS training program. It has strong philosophical ties to welfare legislation in that it reinforces the connection between adult literacy education and work. In fact, this act is included as part of employment and training legislation, as opposed to education legislation. The WIA requires local officials to establish workforce investment boards to create education and training plans at a local level that must be approved by each state's governor. The act places pressure on literacy providers to demonstrate measurable program outcomes and uses three core performance indicators to evaluate programs: (1) demonstrated improvements in literacy skill levels, (2) placement, retention, or completion of postsecondary-education training, unsubsidized employment, or career advancement, and (3) receipt of a secondary-school diploma or its equivalent (Hayes, 1999).

This act also calls for a coordination of educational services with employment services through the creation of what are called "One Stop Career Center Systems." These centers, which are being supported by the Department of Labor, house eighteen federal programs that are required to participate, and a number of state and local agencies and educational institution programs, under one roof. The One-Stops serve as organizing vehicles for transforming an array of employment and training programs into an integrated service-delivery system for job-seekers and employers. These centers also provide information relating to career exploration, the performance of local training providers, and the labor market (U.S. Department of Labor, 1995). At the One-Stops, individuals can go through a single intake process at one location to access a wide range of programs and obtain what is supposed to be seamless service. It is worth noting, however, that TANF is not required to participate in the One-Stops but remains a state and local option.

Additionally, despite federal efforts to provide a system of seamless service to recipients, TANF and workforce education programs remain largely independent and operate as two separate systems. However, with the current emphasis on moving clients quickly into jobs rather than providing cash assistance, the goals and operation of the welfare system are now quite similar to those of the workforce development systems. The systems, although not always under one roof, are both working toward job placement—welfare clients are referred to the various job retraining and education programs and are viewed as job seekers.

The link between adult education and employment has been present since the enactment of the AEA in 1966. This act stated, in part, that its purpose was to "provide adults with sufficient basic education to enable them to benefit from job training and retraining programs, and obtain and retain productive employment" (Grognet, 1997). Other programs that followed, such as JOBS and JTPA, also connected the development of employability skills to adult education programs. These connections received little emphasis. However, they have been greatly enforced as a result of current legislation. The regulations for these programs have been made very explicit in terms of outlining those activities that count in preparing an individual for work and that may be funded with federal monies. The new legislation (including TANF, WtW, and WIA) emphasizes the placement of recipients into jobs in its performance accountability system.

ADULT EDUCATION AND LATINOS

Given these developments, the question remains as to how Latino populations have fared through all of the events and legislation described above. Data that provide numbers of individuals enrolled in adult basic education, GED, or ESL classes that are separated by ethnicity or other characteristics is sparse. The statistics available indicate that Latinos as a group are seeking adult education and training in record numbers. For example, Hispanics were the largest ethnic group served and comprised 53.1 percent of the adult student population during the 1992–1993 academic year in Texas, one of the states with the heaviest concentration of Latinos (Texas Education Agency, nd). In 1999, a national survey sample indicated that a total of 88,809 individuals participated in adult education for a given twelve-month period. This group included 19,491 (22 percent) Hispanics seventeen years of age and older (National Center for Education Statistics, 1999a). Adult education has always served as the safety net for those students who fall through the cracks in our public-school system. Based on the statistics on high-school dropouts, one can infer that the number of Latinos needing adult education is great. It is widely known that our public schools have not served Latino students well—they comprise the largest number of high-school dropouts. These students have the highest dropout rate of any major segment of the U.S. population. In 1998, 30 percent of all Latinos ages 16–24 were dropouts (1.5 million), compared with 8 percent for whites and 14 percent for blacks (White House Initiative on Educational Excellence for Hispanic Americans, 1999). Individuals that are unemployed are frequently the same ones seeking to upgrade their skills through adult education. One figure indicates that 27.1 percent of Hispanic high-school dropouts in 1998 were unemployed (National Center for Education Statistics, 1999b). This provides another indication of the need for adult education among Latinos.

Historically, there has been relatively little effort to meet the needs of Latino non-native English speakers. The AEA provided grants to the states with little guidance regarding the types of programs to be funded. Shortly before the act was reauthorized in 1988, a little less than half of the programs it funded provided instruction in ESL. This instruction was open-ended and usually focused on teaching basic survival skills in English. The reauthorization of the act and the ensuing programs included as their goals the social integration of people with limited English proficiency and the development of employment skills.

There have been some efforts to begin to determine the degree of need among Latinos. Some surveys on the literacy of adult Latinos were initiated within the last fifteen years. The Young Adult Literacy Survey of 1986, for instance, sampled 3,600 persons using a questionnaire translated into Spanish. However, little data could be published regarding Spanish-speaking Latinos given the small number of these individuals in the sample. In 1990 the Educational Testing Service conducted a workplace literacy survey for the Department of Labor that included eight questions related to the respondent's language background. Approximately 2,500 persons enrolled in JTPA and 3,300 persons applying for employment or unemployment insurance benefits took the survey. The NALS survey of 1992 built on these efforts by providing language background questions and oversampling Blacks and Latinos (as the Young Adult Literacy Survey had done) in large urban areas in order to provide data that could be used to report on literacy by race and Latino ethnicity (Macías, 1994). The reports from this survey added much information to our knowledge regarding language diversity in the United States They revealed, for instance, that Hispanic adults reported the fewest years of schooling in this country (an average of a little less than 10 years) among all the racial/ethnic groups. They were also more likely than white students to perform at the lowest two levels of literacy (National Center for Education Statistics, 1996).

ESL instruction has continued as a component of most programs in adult education or literacy. However, as with all other adult education, ESL programs have been severely underfunded and have not met the demand for this type of instruction. An intensive, national effort to provide English language instruction for all federal programs with new funding formulas that would allocate monies to states based on the size of their population of adults with limited English proficiency was recommended over a decade ago by Bliss (1990). This has still not happened. Waggoner (1997) reports, for instance, that according to the National Household Education Survey of 1995, ESL classes served only about 28 percent of the total estimated 2.8 million people who do not speak English at home. Sontag (cited in Gillespie, 1996) reported that in 1990, 17,000 immigrants were on waiting lists for ESL classes in New York City. Consistent with current reports on Latinos as the largest minority group in the United States, she also stated that in 1994–1995, Spanish was the home language for 67 percent of ESL students, or for four of five students participating in ESL instruction or waiting to be enrolled in such classes. Waiting lists indicate that millions of people were looking for ESL classes even before the recent immigration and welfare reform legislation. A report prepared for a national literacy summit indicated that the situation has not improved: "Los Angeles has a waiting list of 50,000 adults for ESOL [English for Speakers of Other Languages]. Most ESOL programs in Chicago are filled to capacity as soon as they open their doors. New York State has resorted to a lottery system to select from individuals who wish to learn English" (National Institute for Literacy, 2000d, p. 11).

Other evidence that indicates that adult literacy has not served Hispanics or the general population well comes from the attrition rate from such programs. Quigley (1997) cited a study from the U.S. Department of Education, indicating that the overall attrition rate for adult literacy programs funded in 1993–1994 was 74 percent. He goes on to say that in order to keep up appearances, educators "explain and rationalize low recruitment levels and high dropout rates in terms that vastly oversimplify program realities and learners' lives" (p. 8).

A current fact report by the National Institute for Literacy (NIFL) adds that nearly 32 million people in the United States speak languages other than English, a 38 percent increase over 1980. Additionally, a policy statement by the institute confirms that more than 50 percent of adults learning English as a second language are Hispanic and account for over 50 percent of adult students (National Institute for Literacy, 2000a). Despite all of these statistics, which overwhelmingly indicate the need for adult ESL instruction, there is a severe lack of services for Latino adults who need to improve their English language abilities. Historically, the lack of English language proficiency has been a major obstacle to the success of workforce education programs for this population, as well as a basis for discrimination against admitting them into such programs.

A study on JOBS participants conducted by the National Council of La Raza in 1995, for instance, found that Latinos were severely underrepresented by JOBS in 7 of 10 states with the largest Latino populations. Even though Latinos represented 17.8 percent of national AFDC recipients at that time, only 12.8 percent of them were JOBS participants. Research indicates that workers with limited English proficiency were often denied entry into JTPA or JOBS programs because of their inability to pass placement tests in English and/or because program officials bypassed them in favor of English-speaking clients with whom the program could show "quick results." When clients with limited English proficiency were allowed into the programs, they were offered ESL classes for such a short duration of time that they could not attain the language skills necessary to enter the vocational part of the program. Thus, they were effectively denied access to education and better paying jobs (Gillespie, 1996). This situation still persists, as discussed in chapter 3.

ADULT EDUCATION POLICY: POLITICS AND IDEOLOGIES

Adult education is currently receiving attention from the federal government, which considers it an integral part of welfare reform. As one report concluded, "Welfare dependency can be reduced two ways: (1) by increasing literacy levels in the general population to reduce the risk of falling into dependency, and (2) by raising the literacy levels of those already on welfare to help them become more financially self-sufficient" (cited in Knell, 1998, p. 10). Yet the current reforms raise several political issues. One has to do with funding. Even though education is seen as the key to self-sufficiency, the rhetoric has not been accompanied with increased monies. Quigley (1997) writes that federal spending in 1991 amounted to $209.35 per adult student. Sticht (cited in Auerbach, 1999) adds that even though enrollment in adult-education programs rose from 37,991 students to over 4 million from 1965 to 1999, 75 percent of the actual dollar amount in funding had been lost. Using the original 1966 value of the dollar, funding dropped from about $274 per enrollee in 1966 to $73 in 1998. The author states, "Taking state contributions into account, funding per enrollee for adult education has grown from around $274 (federal dollars only) in 1966 to $276 (combined federal, state and local dollars) in 1998, about $2 per adult in over 30 years, a rate of growth of less than 7 cents a year!" (p. 1). Apparently, adult education is not a priority.

Latino students are impacted the most by being denied funding in this scenario. They are the students with the largest percentage of high-school dropouts, yet where do the thousands of dollars that are allocated per each dropout go when they leave school? This begs the question of why these dollars are not shifted to adult education, where the safety net can later pick up the many Latinos and other students that drop out of the public-school system. Instead, the system again lets these students fall through the cracks because of inappropriate funding, which in turn makes it impossible to provide the number of classes and qualified staff needed to serve these students.

Another issue has to do with the connection between current legislation, particularly WIA, and literacy levels among those individuals receiving welfare benefits. As stated earlier, the federal government has imposed a Work First approach in welfare reform. The system requires the states to place students in a job as quickly as possible, rather than engage them in education. The link is clear: The purpose of this federal initiative is to save dollars. Yet, the NALS research has also shown that 66 to 75 percent of welfare recipients could not perform tasks at levels 3, 4, or 5 on the survey and, in fact, nearly half of the population scored at the lowest two levels of literacy. There is a major contradiction in this reasoning. Welfare reform emphasizes job placement above education, yet the NALS results indicate that most welfare recipients have literacy skills well below what is required of unskilled laborers and assemblers (Knell, 1998). It is also known that Hispanic adults reported the fewest years of schooling in this country among all racial/ethnic groups (National Center for Education Statistics, 1996). The logical conclusion is that the government is again failing disproportionate numbers of Latinos. They are being pushed into dead-end jobs that do not pay livable wages rather than being provided with incentives to continue their education so that they can acquire a job that can sustain them and their families. The legislation has failed to recognize that education coupled with job training, as opposed to short-term job training by itself, is essential for successful entry into the workforce. The current Work First policy has been described as "promoting 'working poverty' rather than economic self-sufficiency by believing the myth that low-skill jobs provide enough money for families to live on. Without family-supporting wages, it is impossible for recipients to move out of poverty and join the middle class" (Sparks, 1999, p. 17). The research literature (Fisher, 1999) has confirmed that what has developed is a revolving door, where many adults who are placed into jobs return to welfare and/or find themselves unemployed again.

Frequently, what happens is that employers discover a mismatch between the skills required by the job and those possessed by the recipient that they have hired, or the employee finds her/himself in a job that offers no potential for advancement and pays wages with no benefits and at a less-than-subsistence level. A study conducted by the Urban Institute, for example, found that the average wage for welfare leavers is only $6.61 an hour. A full-time, year-round job at this wage amounts to only $13,748 and leaves a family of three at just above the poverty line, which in 1998 was $13,650. Also, only 23 percent of welfare leavers receive health insurance from their employers and more than one-third run out of money for food and rent. Carnevale and Reich (2000) reported that "of the 2.1 million adults who left welfare between 1995 and 1997, 29 percent returned to the welfare rolls by 1997" (p. 14). The General Accounting Office (GAO) also found that the percentage of welfare leavers who returned to the rolls ranged from 19 percent at 3 months to 30 percent at 15 months. A 1999 report indicated that the Hispanic welfare caseload increased by 17.7 percent between 1995–1996 and 1998–1999 (Rodriguez and Kirk, 2000).

D'Amico (1997) has identified an additional problem: a lack of postwelfare assistance. She indicates that of 23 individuals whom she studied, all were still poor and marginalized after welfare because there was no training or educational support to help them with the transition once they were working. D'Amico concluded that welfare-to-work produced employment but did not change lives. The ideology inherent in the current Work First approach to welfare reform is that reducing caseloads and federal dollars spent is more important than reducing long-term poverty—even though the monies that could make a major and positive difference in adult education are only a tiny fraction of the amounts of federal dollars spent in other areas. The U.S. Department of Education spent a total of $385 million on adult education in fiscal year 1999, including $365 million in state grants (U.S. Department of Education, 2000b). On the other hand, one small part of the military budget during that year included 339 F-22 planes ordered by the military at a cost of $187 million each (Center for Defense Information, 1999). The entire spending on adult education was, therefore, equivalent to just a little over the cost of two F-22s. Consider that during the same time period there was an unmet need in the country for food for the hungry. In 1998, the U.S. Conference of Mayors identified low-paying jobs and unemployment as leading causes for increases in emergency food assistance (Peace Action Education, 1999). Rodriquez and Kirk (2000) write that although many welfare mothers are employed, "poverty persists and food insecurity is on the rise" (p. 12).

Another welfare reform issue has to do with federal policy toward single mothers with young children who, under TANF legislation, are expected to work—an issue that has a heavy impact on Latinos. The emotional and physical well-being of parents and children is apparently of lesser importance to the government than saving federal dollars. Fourteen states, for instance, have policies that eliminate the entire family's welfare benefit the first time the mother in the family fails to follow the rules as defined by the

Work First approach (Weil, 2000). Yet, no one is committed to assuring that children of working mothers will be provided with high-quality childcare that is safe and nurturing. Over 90 percent of welfare families are headed by single mothers (Fisher, 1999). Rodriguez and Kirk (2000) further indicate that the number of working-poor Hispanic single mothers from 16 to 64 years of age increased by 18.3 percent to 61,000 between 1996 and 1998, and that the probability of Latinas leaving the welfare rolls to escape poverty appears to be less likely than for their Black or White counterparts. These women are required to enter the labor market within two years even though they cannot afford to pay for childcare. The provisions do not consider that the skills that they have are very different from those of middle-class women in the labor force who earn wages that are high enough to pay for childcare. Additionally, welfare reform permits full-time caregiving when there are two parents but forbids it when there is only one (Sparks, 1999).

The research indicates that Latino families, on average, tend to have more children than white families. In 1997, Hispanics averaged 3.0 births per woman, compared to 2.2 for blacks, 2.0 for Native Americans, and 1.9 for Asian Americans. This trend, furthermore, is expected to continue (National Center for Health Statistics, 2000), as Latinos comprise the fastest growing and youngest segment of the U.S. population (National Council of Latino Executives, 1999). Hispanic single women and children have become a larger segment of the TANF welfare caseload nationally, and because of the additional language and cultural barriers they face are unable to find sustainable employment at wages that allow them to pay for quality childcare. Although WIA and WtW provide subsidized childcare, this assistance can also be problematic for an individual receiving help from more than one stream of funds because of the inconsistency in eligibility criteria across these streams and/or because funding for childcare "runs out" before a student completes a program. A student participating in a focus-group interview on adult education instruction, for example, indicated that she had tuition assistance to continue working on a credential but that childcare monies were no longer available to her. The reality for her, therefore, was that she would be unable to complete the program of study for a certified nurse's assistant license even though she was very close to the end. Thus, again, the legislation has the most negative impact on Latinos, and brings us back to the issue of work versus family. These developments beg the question of what happened to the political rhetoric of "all families being first in America." Why are mothers, particularly, chastised for having latch-key kids or children that find themselves in legal trouble when the federal government, itself, does not allow parents to be at home nurturing and supervising their children or provide adequate monies for childcare? The ideology is that Work First (even though most families are still in poverty) is ultimately more significant than raising productive responsible citizens. Work First also takes priority over the provision for long-term education and training—the only hope for lifting Latinos and all families out of poverty.

These issues lead to another very troubling consequence of the current legislation—the Work First approach has imposed a philosophy on adult education that frequently runs contrary to the personal beliefs of practitioners in the field. Many researchers, educators, and practitioners in adult education hold the belief that the purpose of adult education is much broader than job preparedness. Rather, education is to provide those lifelong learning skills that do not necessarily prepare individuals for any single job but that teach them the reasoning, problem-solving, and critical thinking skills that are required to function successfully in today's society. A common philosophy among practitioners is that the ultimate purpose of education is to bring about social change and positive transformation in people's lives (Cranton, 1997; Mezirow, 1991; Smoke, 1998). The acquisition of a high-school diploma, GED, and postsecondary credentialing is part of this educational development, which will bring about a better job and quality of life. Now adult educators are being asked to push people into jobs knowing that the dead-end jobs that they can fill are not going to lift them out of poverty or advance them towards positive change in their lives. As Sparks (1999) states, "The struggle between ABE [adult basic education] for purposes of social action and change and ABE for individual instrumental growth and economic development is dramatically played out within the arena of welfare reform" (p. 16). Even the best-prepared adult-education administrators and instructors have basically been denied their right to exercise their professional knowledge in the classroom regarding the most appropriate curriculum for their group of students—particularly those that are culturally and linguistically diverse. Most significantly, the work-first approach precludes them from imparting a curriculum that leads learners to question and analyze the social and political order of their lives, to reflect on and to challenge the inequities that surround their current realities.

This situation is not unlike that found in public schools. At the high-school level, for example, classroom practice too often focuses on isolated skills, memory work, and drill. This type of curriculum is neither motivating, engaging, or dynamic, nor does it develop the reasoning, problem-solving, and critical-thinking skills that we want students to develop. In short, it fails to provide an education that prepares youth for postsecondary learning and instead provides, at best, a type of training that teaches students how to regurgitate information, how to retrieve answers to factual questions following a textbook reading, how to take paper/pencil multiple-choice tests, etc. This is particularly true for Latinos, who are often tracked into vocational classes and given no opportunity to enroll in the more rigorous, academic courses (Lucas, 1997). Adult education should provide a second opportunity, or a safety net, for these students to access an education—along with occupational training. Instead, with the push to quickly place their students into jobs, instructors are obligated to reproduce the same type of mechanical skills based curriculum that already failed the students in the public-school system. In short, adult educators are being asked to provide short-term training in lieu of education. Additionally, the time limitations preclude the implementation of a curriculum that develops those cognitive skills deemed necessary for work in jobs that provide an opportunity for advancement.

Another concern is that the current legislation has also denied the voice of the learners, themselves, who are the victims and the ones who could conceivably stand to benefit the most from government-subsidized education and training. Yet, their aspirations, personal, familial, and work-related goals were not considered in the formulation of the current legislation—they were not asked to be a part of this process. This issue of a lack of participation has been raised in forums in the Borderlands by professionals and by workers' associations and groups who have repeatedly testified that their opinions were never solicited, even though it was their fate that legislators were molding through their policies (Border Summit on Adult Bilingual Education, 1998; NAFTA Impact on the Border, 2000). As such, some of the barriers that they face were either not addressed or not adequately addressed in the legislation. Instead, legislation has taken the simplistic view that unemployed and/or displaced individuals are not working primarily because they lack the necessary skills to find a job. While this is certainly a part of the problem, families face many other challenges. Affordable, quality childcare, for example, is not always available or not available for the length of time that is needed in order to complete a program of study for a given credential. Disabilities among parents or children (which make it even more difficult to find childcare) is another problem. Finding affordable housing is an additional barrier. The Center on Budget and Policy Priorities (2000) stated that three-fourths of all poor families on welfare receive no housing assistance and 1.1 million faced severe housing-cost burdens or lived in severely substandard housing. This was problematic, as "the lack of decent affordable housing creates family instability, as families are forced to move frequently, and prevents families from moving closer to areas of high job growth" (p. 6).

Additionally, many workers—particularly women and members of minority groups—face discrimination on the part of employers and training agencies. Schneider (cited in D'Amico, 1999) found in her study of work-training programs that a hierarchy existed where "Latinos were left out of training for the most part" (p. 6). D'Amico (1997) also discovered in her work that there was a double-standard policy among employers for welfare recipients. "Individuals hired from the welfare rolls, as well as almost all the other poor African Americans and Latinos on the staff of the workplace studied, were subject to a completely different set of personnel policies than were other workers. They also received lower wages, no paid sick leave or vacation, and no tuition reimbursement" (p. 20). Melendez (cited in Morales, 2000) confirms that job discrimination against Latinos occurs during the recruiting and hiring processes as well as on the job. Morales (2000) confirms that this is a widespread practice. The lack of proficiency in English among many Latinos most probably contributes to this.

Rodriguez and Kirk (2000) add that in 1999 the Office of Civil Rights (OCR) discovered that several New York welfare offices denied interpreter assistance to persons with limited English proficiency, even sending them home when they did not bring their own interpreter. The OCR also found that bilingual staff members were sparse even in offices that were located within predominantly Hispanic communities. In Oregon, non-English speakers waited four times longer than English speakers for applications in their native language. The result of these practices is the effective denial of services to which Latinos are entitled.

A study by D'Amico and Schnee (1997) in New York City also supports the notion that unemployment issues involve much more than education and training—they include other barriers. The authors found high concentrations of African Americans in public sector jobs and Latinos in manufacturing, making both groups vulnerable to layoffs. The study also determined that program participants who were prepared for better jobs in terms of both English language skills and volunteer experience continued to encounter "a host of political, bureaucratic, cultural, language and economic factors that govern access to jobs" (p. 136). The authors emphasize that noneducational barriers were often the cause of unemployment, and caution educators to be "more vigilant against complicity with the assumption that unemployment can be solved by developing a more literate, English-speaking workforce without addressing the economic crisis and its political origins" (p. 119). Likewise, Hull (1993) in her discussion of popular views of literacy states that an upgrading of literacy skills is too often posited as the solution for employment and for better work performance by workers who are said to be "deficient" and whose lack of "skills" presumably leads to low productivity, poor product quality, workplace accidents, and ultimately—the bottom line for industry—economic losses. Her research has indicated the need to rethink the nature of unemployment and to look more closely at the underlying economic issues.

Although these are societal rather than personal issues, they have been left unquestioned. The recent federal initiatives, rather than taking an in-depth, broader view of the actual (social) roots of the problems of welfare and poverty, focus instead on the relatively superficial issues of training and job placement under the false assumption that a small dose of the former will increase the latter—like a fairy tale, all will have a happy ending (that is, the welfare case loads will drop, people will be back at work, and federal dollars will be saved). However, the opposite is true and, in fact, the fairy tale has turned into a nightmare for many. The nightmare, moreover, has extended to a particular segment of Latinos who seek workforce education because of job displacement. The devastating impact of politics and economics on displaced Latinos has become crystallized in the U.S.–Mexico Borderlands, where additional factors have increased the attention on workforce education issues and added to their complexity.

THE BORDERLANDS REGION

Workforce education in the U.S.–Mexico Borderlands[1] has become a topic of major significance and urgency for two major reasons. The first is that employment and workforce training in the region has been severely impacted by NAFTA. Thousands of workers in manufacturing and related industries have been displaced as a result of this accord, which became effective in January, 1994. The programs that have been set in place to assist these workers have met with little success. Myerson (1997) wrote about the problematic nature of workforce education and retraining programs in the Borderlands:

Even as the nation as a whole is basking in nearly full employment, workers in areas where dominant employers have cut back because of Mexican trade can find themselves living through a depression. While a side agreement to the free trade accord guarantees retraining, the government has no idea how many have found new jobs. Officials call some programs outright failures.

The second reason that workforce education in the Borderlands is a topic of major significance and urgency is that the region presents a unique and often misunderstood situation in terms of the educational, economical, and political issues that are relevant to employment and workforce education. It is only recently that the Borderlands has received increased national attention as the birthplace of what has been called the "Century of the Americas" (Gibbs, 2001, p. 36). A panelist at a nationally sponsored town hall meeting focusing on the border region commented, "The border used to be America's back door, but it's rapidly becoming its front door—where our economic, cultural, and political future is being forged" (Duffy, 2001). Education is also being forged in this area for a large segment of the adult population in the region.

The longest stretch (1,254 miles) of the U.S.–Mexico border is the region bordered by the state of Texas. This area is also the most populated and economically productive part of the border. Nonetheless, a study (Sharp, 1998) that focused on this area found that if the Texas–Mexico Borderlands region (composed of 49 Texas counties) were the fifty-first state in the union it would rank first (among other things) in the following:

• Poverty rate (29.5% in 1993)

- Percent of schoolchildren in poverty (38.0%)
- Percent of the population that speaks Spanish at home (57.1% in 1990)
- Percent of the adult population without a high-school diploma (37.3% in 1990)

The most striking characteristic about the Border region is the high rate of poverty. The per-capita income levels there were consistently less over a 25–year period from 1969 to 1995 than that of the counties served by the Appalachian Regional Federal Commission. Thus, the Borderlands surpass even Appalachia in terms of poverty. Not surprisingly, literacy levels in English are low, considering that a large part of the population speaks Spanish as their native language. Unemployment in 1997 was an average of 8 percent (Sharp, 1998, p. 197). This unemployment rate was twice the rate of non-Border counties in Texas. Furthermore, nine of the border counties had double-digit unemployment rates, four of those with rates above 20 percent. The city of McAllen, Texas, had an unemployment rate of 17.2 percent, which was the fifth highest of any city in the nation (p. 67). Four years later, in 2001, McAllen is still described as "America's poorest city with an average per capita income of $13,333 a year" (Gibbs, 2001, p. 41). Yet, Gibbs points out, it is at the center of the fourth-fastest growing metro area in the United States—a growth spurred by NAFTA.

It is undeniable that education and literacy play a role in the unemployment in the region, given that less than 65 percent of the adult population has a high-school diploma. However, politics and economics are at the root of the problem. There are several highly problematic issues specific to the Borderlands that are a part of the equation: the irresponsible globalization of industry, program eligibility requirements set by government entities, and myopia on the part of all involved regarding the unique characteristics of the Borderland population. Nowhere is this more evident than in El Paso, the largest border city in Texas and the city most affected by NAFTA. The case of El Paso serves to illustrate the complexity of workforce education and unemployment issues as they have evolved in the Borderlands.

NAFTA AND THE TWIN PLANT INDUSTRY

There has been a decline in manufacturing jobs in the United States over the last twenty years. Between 1980 and 1996 there was a ten-point drop in Latino employment in this segment of the labor market (Siles and Pérez, 2000). This was due, to a great extent, to industrial restructuring and globalization. The U.S.–Mexico Borderlands have been greatly affected as a result of these developments. A national survey taken in February, 2000 indicated that a disproportionate number of workers who were employed in manufacturing were displaced (that is, their jobs were lost because the company closed, moved, had insufficient work, or abolished the position), and they comprised the largest share of displaced workers. Approximately 13 percent of the total number of tenured workers (that is, those who had been employed for 3 or more years by the same entity) who were displaced in the three-year period between 1997 and 1999 were of Hispanic origin. Plant closings or moves accounted for 49 percent of worker displacement (Bureau of Labor Statistics, 2000).

Since 1994, NAFTA has directly caused a loss of about 14,500 manufacturing jobs in El Paso. Much of this has been due to the disintegration of the garment industry which for many years was the foundation of the economy. It has indirectly caused the loss of an additional 12,000 jobs including, as examples, services and suppliers (McAlmon, 1999).

The garment industry had an estimated $1 billion affect on the local economy in 1993 and employed 20,600 people. Approximately 1 million jeans were made each year in El Paso and up to 3 million jeans were washed, pressed, inspected, repaired, tagged, folded, bagged, boxed, and shipped annually (Kramer, 1995). Most of the thousands of jobs lost in the apparel and other industries went to Mexico or Asia (Moreno, 1997).[2] The transfer of jobs to Mexico has been so great that the twin plant (or maquiladora industry) there has proliferated from 72 plants in 1967 to 3,500 plants in 1999. Approximately, 400 of these are found in Ciudad Juárez alone—El Paso's twin city on the Mexican side of the border (Cañas, 2000; Padgett and Thomas, 2001). While some employers such as Levi Straus have provided severance packages and other benefits for laid-off workers, many are taking little, if any, responsibility for the basic welfare and re-employment of workers who have been displaced, often with only a few days notice.[3] Rodriguez (2000) writes about the many cases that she, alone, has handled, that involved violation of labor laws by companies who lay off workers, often because they relocate to another country but sometimes because they look for ways to cut back on fair wages. An example of this is a report about a company that did not relocate to Mexico but instead laid off unionized workers and then contracted a smaller number of nonunionized workers to do the same jobs at much lower wages. She adds that these cases often involve a misuse of NAFTA legislative procedures and that laws protecting workers are difficult to enforce. She writes,

Rather than making progress in protecting workers' rights, we appear to be going backwards. That non-payment of wages is still occurring should be unacceptable. That outsiders can come in, rob workers of their wages, and then abscond should not be tolerated. Border workers need protection from this type of exploitation. (p. 3)

A responsible globalization of industry from the perspective of Latino employment in the United States would include, at minimum, full compliance with the Worker Adjustment and Retraining Notification Act (WARN) and subsidies for retraining laid-off workers who had tenure with the company. The argument is made that workforce education and retraining programs have been implemented specifically to assist displaced workers. However, these programs have been fraught with political and economic problems.

EDUCATION AND RETRAINING PROGRAM ISSUES

The issues of education and retraining for those displaced by the changing economy have not been totally overlooked in the past. In 1974, Congress provided for Trade Adjustment Assistance (TAA) to support and retrain workers displaced by economic shifts resulting from free trade. In 1993, when NAFTA was ratified, the NAFTA-TAA (North American Free Trade Agreement Trade Adjustment Assistance) program was created. The purpose of this federally funded program was to provide occupational, remedial, literacy, English-as-a-second-language, and entrepreneurial training, along with income support for up to 52 weeks, payments for job search commutes, and a relocation allowance to employees who lost their jobs because of NAFTA. Workers must prove eligibility for these benefits through certification that qualilfies them as "NAFTA displaced."[4] An additional 26 weeks of income support is available through unemployment insurance, bringing the total to a maximum of 78 weeks (approximately 18 months) of available income to displaced workers through these venues.

Another funding agency is the Texas Workforce Commission (TWC). However, this funding has in the past been inadequate and often discriminatory. For example, even though only 17 percent of TWC funding was received in the Texas border area in 1997, 32 percent of all of the unemployment in Texas could be found in the Borderlands that year. The TWC expenditures for job training on a per capita basis were lower in the Border areas than in the rest of the state. Another example of such discriminatory funding is provided by the Texas Smart Jobs Fund, which awards grants to businesses to train new or existing employees. Although the unemployment rate is generally twice as high in Border counties as in non-Border counties, the region received only 12 percent of grants awarded in 1994–1997 (Sharp, 1998).

A recent report (Texas Border Infrastructure Coalition, 2000) found that in 1997–1998 only 5.3 percent of the eligible population (25 years of age and older) in the state of Texas were served with workforce education programs. The state now ranks second to California in the number of undereducated adult learners (3.4 million) in the United States. A closer look at what has transpired in El Paso illuminates some of the problems. From 1994 to 1997, programs funded by NAFTA-TAA certified[5] almost 7,500 workers in El Paso who had been laid off. In May 1998, El Paso was granted $45 million over three years by the U.S. Department of Labor for setting up workforce centers, and developing and administering retraining programs (including benefits, support services, and economic assistance) for 4,500 NAFTA-displaced workers. (Sharp, 1998). Expectations were that the workforce education systems would be "reinvented" to meet the needs of the displaced workers with these monies. However, the results of two years of implementation of the El Paso Proactive Re-Employment Project (PREP) program, which was set up to administer the grant, indicated that this has not happened, and that the programs that received assistance through the grant were much less successful than anticipated. Templan (2000) describes PREP as "a striking case of a federal program gone awry, and a sad example of the challenge of retraining relatively unskilled workers" (p. 1B).

Of 4,594 workers that participated in PREP over the first two years, for example, 460 (10%) completed basic education or job skills training, while 1,444 (31%) were still taking basic education and 1,098 (24%) were still in job skills training (Kolenc, 2000). Additionally, even though a third-year extension was awarded for PREP, the third year of implementation did not include economic assistance to enrollees. The loss of this modest but vital economic support, which had been provided to workers while in training and education programs, most likely precluded many from continuing and or enrolling in programs.[6] Some preliminary statistics on the outcomes of the program indicated that a total of 3,804 participants had "terminated" the program as of July 2001. Of these, 3,014 entered employment (PREP Program Data, 2001). A breakdown of figures for the third year is not yet available, however, nor is information regarding employment wages and retention for those that terminated the program.

This brings up additional funding issues. One is that many workers cannot survive and support their families on the limited incomes provided during the time they are in training. Also, many workers are required to first develop their English proficiencies within their respective programs before they move on to vocational or other skill-based training. This sequential design is problematic from the economic standpoint because many run out of benefits before they even reach the required levels of English proficiency (Flynn, 1997a).[7] The time limitations set by many of these programs are inadequate to address the educational needs of the population. The eighteen months of benefits provided for displaced workers to learn new job skills, English, and get a GED, when most of them have less than six years of education is simply not enough (Moreno, 1997; Sharp, 1998).[8] A one-size-fits-all program design does not provide the flexibility to meet the complexity of workforce development in the Borderlands. The situation in the Borderlands is not unlike what Merrifield (1997) reported about the women textile workers she studied, for whom "choices are also constrained by family circumstances. Prime among these constraints is income.... Especially for those who are the sole income earner[s], taking time to train, while living on unemployment pay, is not a viable option" (p. 285).

The loss of healthcare benefits, which most often occurs after a job loss, is another significant factor that precludes access to education. Santos and

Seitz (2000) indicate that the rate of insurance coverage for Hispanics is less than that of whites or blacks, and it is lowest among the Mexican-American subgroup of Hispanics. Higher levels of funding in workforce education programs are thus crucial in order to provide much-needed benefits.

Testimonies from displaced workers appearing before the Texas Workforce Commission illustrate the frustration that workers feel as they struggle to complete successfully an education and/or retraining program while not being supported by government entities:

"She said my benefits had finished already. She was asking me what I knew and what I have learned. I told her that I was on the third level of English and it was very slow because when I was in Mexico I only went up to the third grade. I am desperate with a great deal of stress because this situation is provoking me [*sic*] lack of school we had but that does not mean I am ignorant. . . . I think that I have the right like other workers to have training . . . please pay attention to my problem on why I do not qualify because I do not have any more benefits."

"I am desperate because I do not have any money to pay my bills and it's not like I wanted to be unemployed but I would like to move on by getting the education that I need. I have been working here in the United States for twenty-four years."

"The amount I am supposed to get weekly is $92 dollars which is not sufficient in this time since I have serious health problems and this is where all my money has gone towards my health. . . . I am going to keep waiting for help . . . because my necessities will never end." (Border Summit on Adult Bilingual Education, 1998)

Even though there are varied sources of support for these workers, the United States spends far less on training and income support for displaced workers than any other industrialized country (Rosen, 2000). While globalization has, overall, been positive for the country in terms of job growth and productivity, it is the displaced workers in the Borderlands who have had to absorb the negative impact of this industrialization. Additionally, federal government efforts, besides being decentralized and confusing, are not focusing on solutions to this problem, but are rather emphasizing compensation for workers that are laid off. As Rosen (2000) says, federal initiatives are "concentrated on 'compensating the losers' as opposed to preventing plant closings or encouraging the creation of new jobs" (p. 6). Additionally, it is primarily Latinos in the Borderlands who are unfairly carrying most of the burden of trade adjustment for the country. Gibbs (2001) expresses the sentiments of Borderland residents when she writes, "Why should the whole country benefit from the blessings of free trade if the Border region pays the price?" (p. 42).

NEW JOBS FOR THE DISPLACED?

Many of these displaced individuals worked in the manufacturing industry for decades—often for a single company. Now they find themselves not only displaced and without adequate income and healthcare benefits, but also lost and abused by a political and economic system that they feel has, at best, betrayed them. The emotional and financial stresses brought on by this situation have additionally brought severe mental and physical illness to many. Depression, attempted suicide, and a hunger strike have all added to the complexity of unemployment and poverty in the Borderlands. Luz Elena Guzman's (pseudonym) story poignantly presents a case that has become common among workers in the area:

Yo quisiera saber porque el gobierno federal ayuda a las asociaciones e instituciones que solamente han lucrado con nosotros, los trabajadores desplazados, y nos han tratado como personas ineptas.... ¿Por qué a nosotros nos piden el 80% de inglés y el GED, si nunca hemos trabajado con el idioma? Hemos trabajado con nuestras manos. Tengo 27 años trabajando en diferentes compañías textiles.... Me encuentro con mis manos operadas, así se encuentra el 40% o 50% de todos los trabajadores.... Me ha afectado moralmente, porque aúnque yo tenía mis manos operadas, yo desarrollaba mi trabajo ganando $9.50 la hora, y ahora en ninguna compañía me acepta por mis impedimentos.... Me ha afectado fisicamente, porque el estres en el que me encuentro me a estropeado mi salud ... y ahora que no tengo aseguranza, me encuentro constantemente enferma, y los tratamientos medicos estan completamente fuera de mi alcance económico. ... El gobierno federal da los beneficios a programas que han lucrado con nosotros.... Tengo 10 meses sin nada de ingresos que entren a mi casa. ... Tres personas y yo hicimos una huelga de hambre por 15 días, y desgraciadamente con los resultados negativos, nos sentimos usados y vimos que el esfuerzo, porque no nos escucharon, fue en vano.... Señores, por favor tomen conciencia que este es un problema, al cual debemos de tomar decisiones rápidas y prácticas y sobre todo que nos ayuden a salir adelante ... que las companías sean más flexibles y no nos descriminen por no hablar inglés o por no tener el GED o por tener más de 40 años ... por favor tengan conciencia, que somos el 50% de madres solteras. ... ¿Por qué hacernos sentir descriminados, por qué permitir que nuestros compañeros mueran de depresión, por qué permitir que traten de suicidarse? Esto señores, esto es el resultado de NAFTA, el libre comercio. (Guzman, 2000).

[I would like to know why the federal government helps those associations and institutions that have only profited from us, the displaced workers, and have treated us as inept people ...? Why do they ask us for English and for the GED, if we have never had to work with that language? We have worked with our hands. I have worked for 27 years in different textile companies.... I find myself with hands that have been operated on, as do 40 to 50 percent of the workers.... This has affected me emotionally, because even though I had my hands operated on I was still able to do my work and earn $9.50 an hour and now no company will accept me with my impediments.... This has affected me physically, because the stress that I find myself in has ruined my health ... and now that I don't have insurance, I find myself constantly ill, and the medical treatments are totally out of my reach financially.... The federal government is providing benefits to those who have profited from us.... I have been without any income coming into my home for ten months.... Three peo-

ple and myself went on a hunger strike for fifteen days, and unfortunately with negative consequences, we felt abused and we saw that, because they didn't listen to us,
the strike was in vain.... Sirs, please take consciousness that this is a problem where
we must make rapid and practical decisions and above all that you help us come out
ahead ... that the companies be more flexible and not discriminate against us for not
speaking English, nor having the GED, nor being older than forty years ... please
have consciousness, for 50 percent of us are single mothers. ... Why make us feel
discriminated against, why allow our fellow workers to die of depression, why allow suicide attempts? This, sirs, is the result of NAFTA, of free trade.]

It is true that the maquiladora industry has created many new jobs in the
city of El Paso. However, many of these jobs are in middle- and upper-man-
agement, transportation, and finance, or in manufacturing positions in such
industries as metals, plastics, and electronics, which require specific vocational skills, some English fluency, and/or a GED. A 1997 report by the El
Paso Chamber of Commerce reported that a training-gap analysis indicated
that El Paso needed more qualified workers for 5,701 positions available in
these higher-skilled industries (Sharp, 1998). However, these jobs are of little
benefit to many of those displaced workers who are low-skilled and monolingual Spanish speakers, as they require at least enough English language
proficiency to read labels, instructions, operating manuals, and blueprints,
as well as oral language skills that are adequate enough to communicate
with local and out-of-town customers, management, and other workers with
whom they are involved in cross-training on the job (Flynn, 1997b). Many of
the displaced workers do not meet the English requirement for the jobs.

It is true that there are jobs available that do not require a GED or English
proficiency and that pay minimum wage or above—for example, some jobs
in construction, food service, housekeeping, or stocking. However, placing
workers into jobs without facilitating study toward the GED only serves to
place them into the same precarious and vulnerable position they were in before. Murnane et al. (2000) confirm the value of the GED in their study. They
found that dropouts had increased access to jobs and critical work experience with a GED. Of particular relevance to Latinos with low levels of formal
education was their finding that the GED had a positive impact on earnings
for male high-school dropouts who left school with weak cognitive skills.
They state, "For these dropouts, our research shows that acquisition of a
GED improves labor market outcomes by at least 15 percent ... for them acquisition of a GED has a large positive effect on earnings" (pp. 1–2). They additionally stressed that despite the benefits of a GED, it was not enough, by
itself, to lift a family out of poverty, and that the greatest gains were reaped
when the GED credential was used to gain access to college. Still, the possibility of increased earnings is enhanced by the GED. This is illustrated by
data from the state of New Mexico. ABE data for the year 1999–2000, for example, indicate that students with less than a high-school education had an
average monthly income of $492, while those with a high school diploma or

its equivalent earned an average of $1077. The average monthly income, moreover, rose to $1237 with a vocational certificate and to $1670 with an associate's degree (New Mexico State Department of Education, 2001).

Thus, the stop-gap solution of Work First neither addresses the needs of Latinos for an education that will provide them with the key to advancement and growth, nor does it address the vision for a country that promotes education and equal opportunity for all as part of its national goals.

An educated Latino citizenry, moreover, is vital to the growth and prosperity of the United States, particularly given that Latinos constitute a young and sizeable portion of the total population. An education to include literacy development in both English and Spanish is needed to upgrade the labor force skills in the Border areas. (See chapter 3 for a discussion of programs that are implemented in both languages.) Increased funding for these programs could provide for (1) longer periods of time for a program that integrates education, job-skills training, and employment with an opportunity for growth, (2) an increased income during the training time, and (3) continuation of benefits vital to family survival.

In brief, the increased and often irresponsible globalization of industry, the lack of federal efforts to focus on solutions to massive layoffs, discriminatory funding practices for the Borderlands, and limited incomes and benefits during retraining, illustrate the problematic nature of workforce education from political and economic perspectives. However, the curricular design for these programs is still another issue that must be addressed. Curricula must be tailored to meet the needs of the Border population. This has not happened in the past. As mentioned previously, the one-size-fits-all program design that has been implemented has met with little success. Another problematic area in workforce education for unemployed and/or displaced Latinos consists of issues related to curriculum and instruction.

NOTES

1. The Borderlands region that is the focus of this discussion consists of 43 counties along the Texas border; the longest stretch of the 2,000 mile U.S.–Mexico border.

2. The transfer of companies to other countries where they can access cheaper labor brings up a myriad ethical, political, and economic issues having to do with, for instance, the exploitation of workers and the negative impacts of foreign industry on the culture of other countries. However, those issues are beyond the scope of this discussion, which focuses on the education of Latinos on the U.S. side of the border.

3. Even though the Worker Adjustment and Retraining Notification (WARN) Act requires employers with more than 100 workers to give 60 days notice before a plant closing or mass layoff, there are several loopholes in this legislation that employers have used to their advantage. The result is that industry sometimes gives workers as little as a few days notice regarding layoffs.

4. The term "displaced" as per the Bureau of Labor Statistics (1996) refers to those workers "20 years or older who lost or left jobs because their plant or company closed, or moved, there was insufficient work for them to do, or their position or shift was abolished" (p. 1). In order to qualify as "NAFTA displaced" it must be shown that the job that was lost was the result of free trade. The author uses these terms to identify workers and businesses already identified as such in the research literature.

5. NAFTA-TAA certification involves a process whereby a worker is identified as qualified to receive such benefits. The Labor Department certifies a group of workers when a fact-finding investigation determines that increased imports contributed significantly to decreased sales and production and to worker separation in a particular company (Labor Market Information, 1997).

6. Statistics to date indicate that the program outcomes for the third year may be somewhat improved. However, comprehensive data on the program will not be available until October 2001. It appears, for instance, that the actual job placements (approximately 2,558) might exceed the projected placements (2,359) even though the average wage may be lower than projected ($6.91 as opposed to $7.11). Job retention and program completion data will be crucial in determining the actual success of this program.

7. This sequential design is also problematic from the curricular aspect, as is discussed in chapter 3.

8. Some companies offered ESL classes to their employees in previous years while the plants were still in operation. However, relatively small numbers of employees enrolled in these classes. The reasons are not clear, although there appeared to be problems ranging from the level or quality of instruction to the availability of employees during the times that classes were offered. Recent visits by the author to ESL classes at a manufacturing plant, for example, revealed that the foreman would not allow the workers to attend the classes during very busy times—even though the class-time agreement had been negotiated at higher levels. Workers reported that there were times when the foreman would even pull them out of class; thus, these incidences were highly discouraging to worker enrollment in the classes.

3

BILINGUAL PROGRAMS
FOR THE WORKFORCE

Workforce education programs have traditionally consisted of a basic education, literacy, GED, and/or vocational or occupational component. Students, for example, might typically enter a program at the basic skills level where their language and numeracy skills are developed, proceed to a level that further develops their written and oral communication skills, and then enter a job-skills component where a vocation, such as electrical journeyman, is taught. Curricula for these programs is developed in English, and students are expected to have enough English language proficiency to participate in class and to comprehend the textbooks, modules, or other written materials. Latinos who are monolingual Spanish speakers or who have limited English language proficiency have first been placed in ESL classes in order to raise their proficiency to a level where they can comfortably participate in their respective workforce education program.

As discussed in the previous chapter, this traditional paradigm, in which students follow a sequential, linear model of instruction, has met with little success among Latino populations who are unemployed and seeking job retraining and education. This mismatch between traditional programs and Latino student needs, along with the increased emphasis during the sixties on civil rights for minorities, led to a relatively small program in the seventies called the Bilingual Vocational Training Model (BVT). In this model, vocational training immediately began by using both Spanish and English. English language development, or Vocational English as a Second Language (VESL), took place within the context of a specific job. The native language was gradually decreased while the use of English increased. These models were usually implemented by both a vocational teacher and a VESL teacher. BVT resulted from legislation that was passed in 1976 as part of a special funding category of the Carl D. Perkins Vocational Education Act. This was a small, but significant step forward in its attempt to meet the needs of students who were not proficient in English in order to provide them access to program curricula.

Gillespie (1996) described the BVT program models that were developed in the sixties as having had the advantages of providing (a) support for linguistically and culturally diverse students at different levels of English proficiency, (b) vocational training immediately in the native language, and (c) increased amounts of English language instruction as proficiency was developed. On the other hand, some of the disadvantages were (a) the inability to find staff that could teach the vocational areas in the native language, (b) the need to have students in a class who all spoke the same native language, and (c) the need to ensure that students did not rely too much on the native language to the exclusion of English. Nonetheless, a survey that was done in 1984 found that BVT was having a positive impact in that enrollments of limited English proficient students in vocational education programs had increased to 1.3 percent (Gillespie, 1996).

Subsequent Carl Perkins Vocational Educational Act legislation in 1984 also emphasized the recruitment of minority students with limited English speaking skills. In fact, however, studies found that program realities were different; "Most programs continued to use the results of standardized tests to screen out limited English proficient students rather than provide remediation for them" (Gillespie, 1996, p. 27). Approximately ten BVT programs a year were funded at about $150,000 to $250,000 per year from 1976 to 1995, at which time the program was discontinued. Additionally, over the last years, funding for these programs was reduced and the enforcement of regulations to protect the rights of minority students to enroll in vocational education and receive the appropriate services had also been loosened (Friedenberg, cited in Gillespie, 1996).

The majority of existing workforce education programs have followed the traditional model described above, where little or no provision is made for Latinos who are not English-proficient. The result has been failure on the part of many programs to assist Latinos to acquire the education and credentials needed for sustainable employment. This lack of success has been particularly evident in the U.S.–Mexico Borderlands, where thousands of NAFTA-displaced and other unemployed workers have enrolled in workforce education programs only to be frustrated with their lack of progress and continued unemployment and poverty. The traditional, sequential models consisting of basic skills, literacy, ESL, GED, and/or a job-skills component has not met the needs of the mainly Spanish-speaking, middle-aged population, who often have less than six years of formal schooling. Program design is one, although not the only factor, that has precluded higher levels of workforce education success among this population. Current initiatives, such as the Adult Bilingual Curriculum Institute Project (2000) and a study on effective workforce development models (Tondre-El Zorkani, 2001) will provide us with much needed research on instructional programs for the Spanish-speaking workforce.

Several different program models for serving Latinos and other minorities who are not English proficient have been described in the recent literature. These models can generally be categorized into three broad groups as follows: (1) Sequential models that first provide English language development before the student attends training, (2) Concurrent models that offer English language development for part of the day and job skills training during the other part, and (3) Integrated models that combine English language development with job-skills training within a single course (Wrigley, Chisman, and Ewen, 1993). Integrated bilingual program models follow a concurrent model—they offer ESL, job-skills training, and GED during different parts of the day. They are integrated at the program level because students study in all three, or at least in two, components simultaneously rather than finishing one component before starting another. Bilingual workforce education programs build on the principles of bilingual education, although the models are necessarily different from those existing in public-school education. The adult student clientele brings a different set of educational circumstances to the classroom—including, for example, tight time constraints, extremely diverse levels of formal education and of literacy in both the native language and English within cohorts, lower motivation levels, the need for support services such as transportation and childcare, and financial pressures. These circumstances preclude the replication of successful bilingual-education public-school models with adults seeking workforce education. The characteristics of some workforce education programs, such as open-entry, open-exit policies, add to the complexity of educating Latinos who need to develop English language proficiency. The basic principle underlying K-12 bilingual education of providing instruction in a language that is comprehensible to the student, and providing equal access to curricula is, however, equally applicable to workforce education. Without bilingual instruction, workforce education is essentially marginalizing a large segment of the population that is most in need of such services.

BILINGUAL EDUCATION

Funding for bilingual education programs in public schooling was first authorized in the United States in 1965 under the Elementary and Secondary Education Act. The purpose of these programs was to meet the needs of those considered "educationally deprived children," who did not speak

English as their native language. The intent was to teach these children subject matter in a language that they understood, while also gradually teaching them English until they were able to make a transition into all-English instruction. These programs were supported by legislation such as *Lau v. Nichols*, which established in 1974 that language programs for language minorities not proficient in English were necessary to provide equal educational opportunities (Baker, 1996). Since then, bilingual education programs have proliferated throughout this country and have only recently been challenged in states such as California and Arizona, where voters have approved legislation that blocks bilingual instruction in favor of all-English instruction for public-school students. Multiple research studies (Collier, 1992; Crawford, 1991; Faltis and Hudelson, 1998; Krashen, 1996; Ramirez, 1992) have documented the success of high-quality bilingual education in promoting academic achievement among students as well as literacy in both English and the native language. Successful programs have various distinguishing characteristics, such as ongoing professional development for school staff, adequate materials in the native language, a transition to all-English instruction in the later rather than earlier grades when students have achieved higher levels of native language development, and community support for the program.

The more recent dual-language programs provide second-language instruction for all students in the program. Native English speakers are provided instruction in Spanish or another language, while non-native English speakers are provided instruction in English. However, there is no single model of bilingual education. In fact, one typology (Mackey, cited in Baker, 1996) of bilingual education programs reported ninety different patterns of bilingual schooling. Thus, although the term "bilingual education" sounds simple, it in fact refers to a complex process. One definition that applies to all programs is that bilingual education uses two languages as the medium of instruction, and it is this same description that is the one common factor among current bilingual workforce education programs.

A basic theoretical principle underlying public-school bilingual education is that of the transfer of knowledge. Conceptual knowledge that has already been acquired in the native language will transfer to the second language—only the corresponding language in the second language needs to be learned. When the ability to gather, use, and analyze information is learned in Spanish, for instance, it does not have to be retaught in English. Likewise, literacy and numeracy skills—such as writing a business memo or figuring the area on a wall that is to be painted—learned in the native language need not be relearned in English. Instructional time can instead focus on developing the language proficiency required to be able to complete those tasks in English and not, for example, on teaching the difference between informal and more formal business language, the appropriate format for a memo, or how to compute the area of a plane.

These principles apply as well to bilingual workforce education. Those workers who come in with certain literacy, numeracy, and occupational skills in their native language can progress more quickly through a program that uses Spanish to build on the conceptual knowledge they bring with them. They can also more quickly develop new understandings in the respective program components, such as GED instruction and/or office skills. Concepts are simultaneously reinforced in the ESL or Vocational English as a Second Language (VESL) component of a bilingual program, as English is developed using the content that was taught in Spanish. The integration of at least some program components thus allows a student to advance in all areas: English language development, GED instruction, and vocational training and education. This integrated model has been implemented across diverse programs and has experienced success in terms of student program completion, acquisition of credentials, and job placement. The Borderlands, particularly, have been at the forefront in terms of the development of current bilingual workforce education programs. Bilingual instructional models have recently been developed there specifically to serve Latinos with diverse levels of formal schooling and literacy skills. Figure 3.1 presents an integrated bilingual program model of workforce education for Latinos that is promising, as evidenced by data from programs that operate at three levels: the Center for Employment Training (CET) at a national level, Motivation Education & Training, Inc. (MET) at a multistate level, and AnaMarc Educational Institute at a local level. All three of these programs implement bilingual instruction in the models they have developed for Borderland Latinos.

CENTER FOR EMPLOYMENT TRAINING

The Center for Employment Training (CET) model, which originated in San Jose, California, has the long-standing reputation of a "program that works." It is also the program that seems to have the longest history—it was founded in 1967 by a Franciscan priest who later served as the first chairman of the board of directors until his death in 1996. This program was born as a result of the farm worker's movement in the sixties and the lack of access to employment experience by displaced farm workers and other poor populations. It is unique in that it was conceived and designed by social activists who were totally committed to helping those segments of the population who were marginalized from the economy. This sense of commitment, caring, dedication, and social justice continues as the primary characteristic that exudes from an organization whose mission is to "train economically disadvantaged individuals for entry-level jobs that are permanent, not subsidized, and frequently offer a benefit package and the opportunity for career advancement" (Meléndez, 1996, p. 29). CET was recognized by the Department of Labor as early as 1971 for being the only

Figure 3.1
Bilingual Instructional Model for Workforce Education

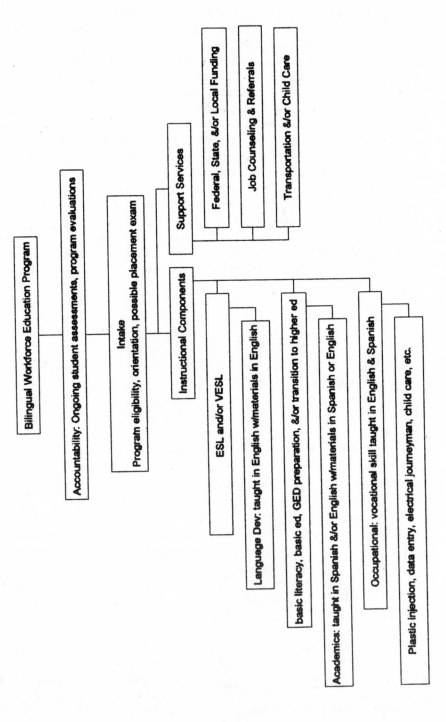

program that made a significant impact on students by increasing their annual earnings by 33 percent, or $7,342, a recognition that prompted the provision of funds to CET for establishing replication centers throughout the country. This compares with other programs that have as little as a $400 increase in earnings per year (Claiborne, 1993). The program, moreover, is seen as cost-effective—tuition per student remains under $7,000. Students are funded through multiple grants and federal job programs. CET has an ethnic mix of students—however, the majority are Mexican-American. Programs are offered bilingually only in regions where Spanish language instruction is appropriate, such as in the Southwest.

The integrated program model features an open-entry, open-exit, variable course-length format. Students train individually, at their own pace, using competency-based curricula that are mostly developed by CET in collaboration with employers. Learning is contextualized and emphasizes real-life applications with much hands-on experience using the same modern equipment that is used in industry. The vocational areas that are taught vary according to each center and according to local labor-market demands in each region. Some of the areas taught include automated-office skills, commercial food services, automotive mechanics, sheet-metal fabrication, and computer-aided drafting (Lee, 1995). Instructors have a minimum of five years of experience (although most have much more) working in the occupational area they teach. The strong relationships with employers that CET has established over the years is one of its distinguishing characteristics and is seen as most responsible for its success. Employers have ownership in the program in that they collaborate in the development of the curricula. They also participate in the program by hosting field trips to the work sites and internships for students. Additionally, the instructors, who themselves were working in industry and had risen through the ranks prior to transferring to CET, provide another link to employers. They have well-established contacts and are also intimately familiar with the work environment and expectations from different companies (Meléndez, 1996).

The center in Socorro, Texas, serves as an example of a CET bilingual program. The enrollment for this center is generally between 27 and 80 students, most of whom have six years or less of schooling and are literate in Spanish. The students are in class for six hours per day, Monday through Friday. The students are following integrated curricula that includes occupational training in either truck driving or warehousing (the two areas offered by this particular center), and VESL. The curricula is customized by the center, with the exception of some supplementary books and materials for teaching English. Students are also studying for their GED. However, this is a separate program that takes place after school hours, from 3 to 4 P.M. daily. The GED is offered in both languages with materials provided in English or Spanish, and the instruction is provided in both English and Spanish so that it is comprehensible to all students. The instructor does not translate but rather uses both languages, alternately and as needed, to explain diverse concepts to groups with diverse abilities in English and Spanish. GED instruction is offered for 21 and 24 weeks, to coincide with the length of instruction for the warehousing and truck-driving programs, respectively. Toward the end of the programs, students take the GED practice tests, and if deemed ready they then proceed to register for the official GED exam. Additional GED instruction is offered by CET in the various exam areas for those students who do not pass one or more portions of the exam.

The center offers all training materials in English or Spanish (except for VESL), so that the students can opt for the language in which they are most comfortable. All the staff at the center, except for one truck-driving instructor, are bilingual. Small-group instruction is provided as part of the curricula, and this instruction is done bilingually, using both Spanish and English as needed. There is no assessment when students enter the program; however, the first ten days of a student's enrollment are seen as a trial period to see if there is a good match between the student and the program. A referral process is in place for students who might be better placed in a different program, and "remediation" is done for those students that need to further develop their literacy skills in order to succeed. Competency exams are given as students proceed through the instruction. A team approach is used—all the staff (instructors, job developer, director, counselors, etc.) guide and assist the students with their studying. The team has regular "unit meetings" in order to determine how to best help the students succeed and which roles each team member will take. The counselor, for instance, will meet with a student who is having problems with, for example, childcare, transportation, or finances, in order to help them solve these problems and complete the program. Most students finish within six months, although some will take as long as ten months depending on their skill levels at entry and on whether they experience any familial or other problems that keep them from concentrating on their training. The success rate is high: approximately 80 percent of the students pass their GED, and approximately 88 percent and 76 percent are placed in truck-driving and warehousing jobs, respectively.

Although the center was without a job developer at the time, the director indicated that employers' relationships with CET were so well-established that job placement was not a problem. As with all their other centers, the culture in Soccoro is one that prepares students for the rigors of work. The setting simulates a work environment. Students punch time cards as they come in and leave, instructors are seen as supervisors, and the training is seen as a job. Yet, amidst this there is a definite culture of caring and dedication in the organization, where every student's success is seen as every staff member's goal. Students sense this and become more motivated to complete. It is not unusual for "graduates" to come back to the center to visit and share their success stories. One couple who came back recently, for instance, shared that they had done well enough to now own two trucks of their own. Another shared that he had advanced in the warehousing business to the point of now making $16 per hour (S. Avila, personal communication, January 29, 2001). The success at this center echoes the program's motto: "Sí se puede" (It can be done).

MOTIVATION EDUCATION TRAINING PROGRAM

The Motivation Education Training Program (MET) is a private non-profit organization that operates in four states: Texas, Louisiana, North Dakota, and Minnesota. The focus here is on the Texas program, which serves high numbers of Latinos through its eleven field offices and numerous other entry points throughout the state. MET's migrant-and-seasonal-farmworker career-development program is funded by the U.S. Department of Labor and has been in operation, in one form or another, since 1967. The mission of MET is "to provide academic and vocational training to migrant and seasonal farm workers, and their qualified family members, with the objective of furthering economic self-sufficiency" (MET, Inc., nd, p. 1). To this end, the program also provides support services as needed, such as low-income housing development and rehabilitation, and comprehensive child and family development services for rural residents through Head Start. There are several eligibility requirements for the program. Primary among these are that workers must have earned a minimum of 50 percent of their earned income from farmwork, that they should have earned at least $800 from agricultural employment, and must have worked only periodically throughout the year. Additionally, male participants born after 1960 must be registered with the selective service (G. Flory, personal communication, February 14, 2001; MET, Inc., 2000).

MET offers three basic components in their training system: Classroom Training, On the Job Training, and Work Experience. The Classroom Training part of the system offers ESL, occupational instruction, ABE, GED, postsecondary transition, and an array of other academic programs. The On the Job Training involves agreements that are made with specific companies to train and hire those clients who may already have limited nonagricultural job skills. MET will pay up to one-half of their salary—contingent upon required qualifications. It is expected that the company will hire the employee permanently if the training is completed successfully. The Work Experience component places clients with few or no skills outside of agriculture with employers who will provide workplace skills. MET pays the complete costs for this training in addition to paying for support services that are necessary for the client to complete the program. The individual components offered by MET can also be combined in order to offer comprehensive services, as needed, to every client. The ultimate goal of MET is to place clients in unsubsidized permanent employment in a job that pays sustainable wages and that provides opportunities for advancement in both earnings and responsibility. A distinguishing characteristic of MET is that the program collaborates very closely with industry for job placement both during and upon completion of the training and provides follow-up services for up to a year after employment to make sure that the transition is successful (G. Flory, personal communication, February 14, 2001).

The El Paso program serves as an example of how MET is implemented with bilingual or Spanish monolingual populations. This program serves anywhere from 100 to 300 workers per year, and virtually 100 percent of the clients are Latino. A new class begins about every five months, with the program for any one cohort lasting between five and seven months. Students enrolled in the program enter with diverse literacy and numeracy skills. The most recent year indicated that in the El Paso office approximately 79 percent of the clients had completed only the eighth grade of school or less, a figure that is considerably below the statewide average of only 30 percent of clients having completed the eighth grade or less. There is also a marked contrast among the Borderland population—many more are identified as having low levels of English proficiency. In El Paso, 83 percent of clients were identified as having limited proficiency in English compared to 31 percent statewide. Another interesting characteristic among MET's El Paso clients is that only 5 percent receive public assistance, as compared with 12 percent statewide.

The occupational areas that are provided vary depending on the interests of the participants and on the opportunities available in the local job market. Areas that have been offered in the past include electricity, computers, warehousing and materials handling, and basic-care attendant (including the certified nursing assistant certificate). There are three components to the program: the GED (240 hours of instruction), vocational training with a capstone course that simulates the actual job experience (hours vary depending on the area; plastic injection molding is 136 hours), and VESL instruction (240 hours). A remediation course lasting 96 hours is provided prior to beginning GED instruction for students with very low literacy and numeracy skills (V. Urquidi, personal communication, February 5, 2000).

The program is bilingual, with all materials available in Spanish and English. GED instruction is generally provided in Spanish and takes place for eight hours a day, five days a week. Upon completion of this program (after approximately 7 weeks) students take the GED exam. After taking the GED, the students begin the vocational and English language courses, both of which are integrated. Students who do not pass the GED are referred to another GED preparation course (outside of MET) or are placed in the GED component again after they complete the VESL and plastics training so that they can continue studying and repeat the exam. In any case, all of the students are allowed to continue with the VESL and occupational parts of the program. The occupational aspect of the instruction includes much hands-on experience and other instruction that is provided bilingually. The VESL component focuses on the language that is used at the work site, including, for example, names of equipment, the identification of defective parts, and the identification of processes. The local community college is the provider for most of the MET training. Students in the program are given a stipend of $5.15 per hour for eight hours per day, plus school tuition, books, and mileage if they live more than 50 miles round trip from the classroom. In order to replace possible income that is lost due to participation, the stipend is paid for as long as the student is in the program. The job placement rate is impressively high. In El Paso, 97.8 percent of the clients were placed during the most recent year. This, despite the fact that 62 percent of them were characterized as having multiple barriers to employment, and 62 percent had been long-term dependents on the agricultural labor market (G. Flory, personal communication, March 8, 2001; V. Urquidi, personal communication, February 16, 2001).

The instructional and administrative staff provide counseling to the participants and any other assistance needed to overcome any barriers to completion of the program. The program is small and personal; the staff members are familiar with all of the students on a first-name basis and communicate with them frequently as they monitor their progress, provide needed support services, and/or refer them to the appropriate social service agencies. There is a strong emphasis in the program on personalized attention for every participant, and the staff is highly dedicated to making sure that the students complete the program (V. Urquidi, personal communication, February 16, 2001).

Some of the parents that are participating in the program have children who have also worked in the fields. These students generally come in with higher levels of skills and/or with work experience in different areas. MET offers these individuals a program where they are provided with some classroom training and/or placed in a job for up to three months (usually in an office) for On the Job Training. Half of their salary may be paid by MET with the expectation that the employer will be satisfied with the worker and hire him or her permanently at the end of the three-month period—they are almost always hired. The philosophy at MET is that the job training and placement is seen only as a means to an end; it provides some financial security for the family. The staff encourages all participants to continue their education. Some students have in fact been greatly encouraged by their success in learning and have continued going to school at night after completion of the program. An additional incentive is that the program pays for their last year of college if they qualify based on income and some agricultural work. This program has enjoyed much success, based on job placement and an increase in earnings.

The average farm worker earns $3,185.00 per year; their salary is often tripled once they begin working in an occupational area. Kolenc (1998) reported that in 1997, 165 migrant and seasonal farm workers went through the plastics operator program and 77 percent of them found a job in the plastics industry raising their average annual salary from a little over $3000 to approximately $10,000 a year. Clearly, MET is fulfilling its mission of improving the lives of workers and their families.

ANAMARC EDUCATIONAL INSTITUTE

The Anamarc Educational Institute opened its doors in April, 2000 and operates locally in El Paso, Texas. Although new, this program also offers a promising model that is bilingual and integrated. The school mainly serves monolingual Spanish speakers with an average education of two to six years in Mexico. Some are illiterate in their native language. Approximately 70 percent of the 81 students who are enrolled are NAFTA-displaced workers who had been working for decades in the garment manufacturing industry—100 percent of them are Latino, mainly of Mexican descent. The institute is committed to high educational excellence in its four-pronged mission, which consists of (a) preparing learners for a competitive bilingual and bicultural workforce in the Upper Rio Grande region, (b) placing graduates in the targeted fields for which they were trained, (c) increasing students' English proficiency, and (d) preparing them to pass the GED. An overall goal of the institute is to encourage all of their students to pursue higher education upon completion of their year-long training. The institute is distinctive in its philosophy that the occupational training is only a stepping stone that brings families some financial security so that the worker can continue his or her education. The entire management and educational team at the school is bilingual, and all are full-time, including the instructional staff. The school offers customized training to students in four occupational areas: childcare worker, computer data entry, phlebotomy technician, and medical assistant. Each of these programs integrates instruction in ESL and GED so that students study in all three areas simultaneously rather than sequentially.[1] As part of their program of study, students participate in mandatory externships, field trips to work sites, and much hands-on training provided by instructors, all of whom have a minimum of three years' experience in the area they are teaching. The program length is twelve months, and employment assistance is provided upon completion. ESL, GED, Spanish as a second language (SSL) and Spanish literacy are also offered to students as stand-alone programs (Houde, 2000a).

Students in the program attend classes Monday through Friday from 8:00 A.M. to 3:30 P.M. Approximately three hours a day are spent in the occupational area, 2.5 hours in ESL, and 1.5 hours in GED. GED instruction is provided in Spanish, ESL instruction is all in English once students get past the early beginner's stage, and the occupational classes are bilingual. The instructors in the occupational classes use different degrees of Spanish and

English when speaking to their students, as appropriate. The textbooks in these same areas are all in English, and the instructor paraphrases, summarizes, and/or discusses the material from these books using Spanish and some English—again depending on the proficiencies of the particular group being taught. Students are evaluated for placement in the ESL classes upon entry into the program by both standardized exams and a one-on-one interview. They are also given a GED pretest in Spanish at that time in order to assess their skills in the content areas covered by that exam (A. Houde, personal communication, January 25, 2001).

The program offers personal assistance and counseling to any students facing barriers to completion. The institute, additionally, offers a warm, friendly, caring, and nurturing environment in which the entire staff always makes a concerted effort to motivate the students to complete their courses and to continue their postsecondary education. Part of this effort involves a readiness on the part of the staff to offer one-on-one assistance as much as is needed when students are having problems learning any of the material. The director of the institute makes herself personally available to all students. She greets students by their first names on a daily basis as she walks through the halls and visits classes, making sure that everything is in order. Additionally, she maintains an open-door policy in her office to all staff as well as students. The atmosphere throughout the institute is familial, bicultural, and bilingual, characteristics that are apparent from the time one walks into the building.

Anamarc Educational Institute maintains a strong system of accountability and collects quantitative as well as qualitative data on all students. Comprehensive data from the first year of implementation will be available in the fall of 2001. Preliminary data indicates that the school is fulfilling its mission of preparing students in the occupational, GED, and ESL areas. Data from the first quarter of operation shows that students' scores on the GED practice test went up by more than 12 points, from 41.04 to 53.90 (Houde, 2000b). Second-quarter results for the institute indicated that of 16 students who took either the mathematics, writing, or literature portion of the GED, 14 (88%) passed the given exam. The ESL data from the second quarter indicate that one cohort of students that began with a foundations class gained 7 points on the ESL exit exam from the beginning of the first quarter to the end of the second quarter. A second cohort that began in second quarter had gained a total of 15 points by the end of that quarter. A major accomplishment in the vocational area is that all eleven students who were in the medical assistant class took and passed their national certification exams in the summer of 2001. Thus, while the evaluation data on this new program has not yet been compiled, it appears by the indicators to date that it is very successful in terms of student progress. It is certainly a promising model.

CET, MET, and the Anamarc Educational Institute present promising models that are implementing bilingual instruction and that are experiencing success. However, they can be strengthened to better meet the needs and interests of learners. All three models, for instance, need additional time in order to better prepare their students for the GED exam. For example, of 275 students In the MET program who took the GED from July 1996 to the present, 127 (46 percent) passed and 148 (54 percent) failed. Additional time would be needed to raise the educational skills of the students so that a greater percentage would pass the exam. Yet, program administrators are restricted by the timelines established by federal assistance programs that provide tuition and support services for their students. Therefore, they must limit the time spent on the various components in order for workers to complete the program. The result is that some are left without that credential that is so necessary for many jobs—a GED—because the instructors did not have enough time to prepare them for the exam, and they consequently failed it.

There are other areas, such as increased pedagogical knowledge about bilingual instruction for adults and staff development, that would greatly enhance these programs. Nonetheless, all three models have a solid foundation on which to build. They have already made great strides by designing programs that use both English and Spanish in the classroom, as well as by creating a caring atmosphere in which the staff members have taken on personal commitments to help their students succeed. All three programs have great potential.

BILINGUAL INSTRUCTION IN THE ADULT CLASSROOM

As indicated in previous chapters, the legislative constraints placed by funding agencies and government entities on unemployed or displaced workers seeking job retraining and/or an education preclude or, at best, discourage the implementation of study programs necessary for placement in better-paying jobs with advancement opportunities. It is incumbent upon all administrators and educators working with adults to advocate for increased benefits that permit education and support services for a duration of time that will allow them to obtain a GED and a postsecondary credential. It is also the responsibility of educators to design programs that best meet the needs and interests of learners and that will place them in jobs with an opportunity for growth. However, the vision of education for Latinos must not be lost. Continuing education can be integrated into long-term programs of study that are coupled with full-time employment. The possibility of transition to higher education must also not be overlooked as a long-term goal.

The issue of the language or languages of instruction in a workforce education program thus becomes fundamental for Latinos. Bilingual instruction becomes essential if programs are to retain students long enough to complete an education that is potentially transforming in terms of job placement and advancement. This chapter has presented some promising bilingual instructional models that are currently being implemented in English and Spanish. Because the majority of the students that these programs are serving are Spanish-dominant, the programs generally provide GED instruction in Spanish, VESL, or ESL instruction primarily in English, and occupational training bilingually. The materials that are used are also in Spanish and/or English. These programs are sound—they allow students to further develop their native-language literacy before or simultaneously with bilingual and/or ESL instruction and, therefore, acquire skills in the native language that will transfer to English (Baker, 1996; Rivera, 1999a). The teaching of subject matter in Spanish is also pedagogically sound, for conceptual knowledge must be developed in a language that is comprehensible to students. Conceptual knowledge that is learned in the native language also serves as a source of skills transferable to English. It appears then that occupational skills and related conceptual knowledge (including, for instance, problem-solving and team management) are best taught in Spanish and supplemented with instruction in English, which supports more concrete, discrete learning (such as names of processes and equipment). The ESL or VESL component of instruction should integrate the development of the multiliteracies and critical thinking described earlier. This implies that the use of some Spanish may be necessary, particularly at the beginning levels, for the development of critical thinking demands that instructors engage student understanding of class-generated themes. The use of the native language in beginning ESL classes in order to make them accessible to beginning-literate Spanish speakers has been supported in the research literature. The use of the first language, for example, reduces affective barriers to learning, allows for clarification of abstract concepts, facilitates classroom management, and facilitates the discussion of cross-cultural issues, power relations and other themes that develop critical thinking (Auerbach, 1993). It is imperative, however, that English language instructors remain focused on the development of English and use Spanish consciously and as needed. As professionals, they must use their expertise and not cross that fine line into the consistent use of Spanish in the class. In no case should instructors use translation to Spanish on a consistent basis in the ESL class.

Models have been described for bilingual workforce education programs, where the components of the program are taught in Spanish and/or English—thus, the program is bilingual in nature. However, there is no existing model for what bilingual instruction actually looks like within a single adult-education classroom. The research that will result from projects such as the El Paso Adult Bilingual Curriculum Institute (2000) may provide such models in the future. There is, however, a strong body of research literature on the use of two languages for teaching and communication that provides some insights into the effective use of two languages among bilinguals.

LANGUAGE USE IN BILINGUAL INSTRUCTION

The issue of language use in bilingual education as relevant to public school instruction has been explored for decades. The language(s) that are used in such programs are key to the program model that is implemented. Bilingual education, for instance, may be characterized as following an alternate-days model (where Spanish and English are used on alternate days), or as a subject-allocation model (where certain subjects are taught in English and others in Spanish). The issue of language distribution within a single class, however, is much more nebulous. Much less research has been conducted that relates to how a teacher actually uses, or distributes, two languages for instruction within a single lesson. Nonetheless, there is a body of research literature in this area stemming from the early seventies until the present time that focuses on language distribution issues in bilingual instruction. Although this research was done within the context of public-school instruction, the principles are applicable to adult education and can inform instruction in this field. There are currently no guidelines that tell an instructor how to use Spanish and/or English in adult bilingual education, even though some models such as those described earlier in this chapter utilize bilingual instruction within certain program components—for example, in the occupational areas, the GED component, and to a lesser extent in the VESL components. The instruction has been generally characterized as a type in which the languages are alternated in order to make sure that the students comprehend the subject matter. But what is involved in this alternation? The research that can inform adult bilingual instruction focuses on the concurrent use of two languages in instruction.

The early literature in the area of concurrent language use focused on two areas: the syntactical patterns of switching between Spanish and English in the discourse of bilinguals, and the sociolinguistic patterns of such switching (Barker, 1972; Huerta, 1978; Pfaff, 1979; Poplack, 1980). Later studies evolved from this body of work that applied and extended the findings to classroom instruction. Studies in bilingual classroom instruction focused on the teaching of subject matter, such as social studies or science. These studies found three patterns that were typically used in bilingual classes:

- Random switching from one language to the other—the teacher would essentially switch within sentences or between several sentences of the same thought group with no language consistency whatsoever

- Consistent alternation, or translation, between English and the students' native language, so that everything would be said twice
- Use of the native language to preview a unit to be taught, followed by in-depth teaching of the unit in English, to end with a review in the native language

A fourth pattern that was deemed to be more innovative and was called the "new concurrent approach" was later explored. This approach was basically described as follows:

- The language alternation occurs mainly between thought groups and is only teacher-initiated and consciously and strategically used; there is no switching within sentences (Jacobson, 1990)

The first type of language alternation is most typically used among bilinguals who are engaged in informal dialogue, where the switching of languages is often subconscious but plays a strategic role. The switch to one or the other language, for instance, may signal emphasis, a change in the person that is addressed, or a change in topic (a school-related topic might signal a switch from Spanish to English, for example). The high level of inconsistency in this approach makes it undesirable for instruction as it precludes any control over the relative amounts or frequency with which each language is used. Such an approach also precludes the conscious use of one language or the other to develop literacy, biliteracy, and/or to ensure comprehension of content. The second type of language alternation involves a very conscious use of translation. This approach demands a highly bilingual individual who has command of both languages across different domains and styles. Such an individual would be able to use either language in formal or informal social situations, or in contexts ranging from familial subject matter to academic subject matter. This approach becomes quite tedious and lengthy for classroom use. Moreover, students tend to tune out when the weaker language is being used, so that classroom time is not effectively used.

The third and fourth approaches, where the languages are used strategically, appear to have more application to bilingual instruction in workforce education programs. In occupational academic classes, where the goal is the learning of content, student understanding is what should drive language use. Thus, the stronger language (Spanish, for many Latinos) would be best used when explaining the role of play in the language and social development of a child in a bilingual occupational class on childcare. English might be used in such a class when demonstrating the use of different store-bought as well as home-made toys and games that promote interaction among children. Likewise, the instructor might switch to the stronger language in a medical-assistant class when explaining the interpretation of rules having to do with patient rights or ethics in the field. English might be used when demonstrating how to draw blood or when explaining how to mount the EKG readings on a board for reading by the doctor. The notion that is applied here is that the stronger language is best used when the context is one that is more cognitively complex and where there is little or no visual support. The alternate, or developing language, might be best used when the topic of discussion is less complex and/or more discrete in nature, and when there is some support either through visuals, objects, or student interaction in the classroom. This notion is supported by research in bilingual instruction and second language instruction that has demonstrated the effectiveness of these principles (Baker, 1996; Garcia, 1990; Rodríguez, Ramos, and Ruiz-Escalante, 1994). Garcia's (1990) study of language distribution in a bilingual classroom states that a significant instructional feature in successful classrooms "was the particular way in which the two languages were combined. Teachers . . . mediated instruction . . . by using the students' native language and English for instruction, alternating between the two languages whenever necessary to ensure clarity of instruction" (p. 107).

Instruction in the students' native language is also optimal when the topic of discussion draws on the students' cultural background. A discussion of the importance of storytelling for children in a childcare class, for instance, might draw on student memories, the stories students were told by grandparents or other family members, and the social context in which they were told. Use of the language in which the students experienced the events under discussion facilitates self-expression as well as creative expression in the classroom, thus providing for richer and livelier dialogue and, ultimately, improved learning. This notion can also be applied to ESL or VESL classes. In explaining a particular grammatical feature or an appropriate use of formal versus more informal styles of language, for example, the instructor might draw on the students' knowledge of comparable features in the native language.

A question that arose in the study of the new concurrent approach (Jacobson, 1990), had to do with whether the alternation of languages within a class, as opposed to the strict separation of languages by subject matter, might not lead the students to mix the languages to a point where the development of one or the other language would be impeded. The results of the study found that this was not the case when the languages were alternated carefully as opposed to randomly. "The unproven hypothesis that children will mix the languages when taught in a language alternation mode was rejected, at least when the latter is, as in NCA [new concurrent approach], a carefully structured concurrent approach" (p. 15). While this study applied to children, it is even more unlikely that language alternation would impede language development in adults who already, at minimum, have high levels of oral language development in the native language and varying levels of development in English. Other work that has focused on bilingual adults who demonstrated an extensive amount of language switching in their discourse, moreover, indicated that when appropriate, these adults separated the languages (Huerta, 1978; Silva-Corvalán, 1983).

Observations of adult education classrooms reveal, however, that the alternation of languages is not always conscious and structured. The subconscious use of two languages in the classroom also plays a vital role in learning and is a strategy that is used frequently by instructors. The switching of languages is also used for functions such as creating a social context that is comfortable for the student, establishing rapport between instructor and student, and drawing attention to a specific point when needed. These observed uses of language alternation are congruent with what previous studies have found. Research (Barker, 1972; Huerta, 1978; Silva-Corvalán, 1983; Tim, 1993) on language alternation among bilingual adults found, for example, that there were several factors that trigger a switch from one language to the other:

- Elaboration—when additional information or details on a topic were added

- Emphasis—when the instructor stressed or underscored a point

- Clarification—when the instructor switched languages to paraphrase a specific point

- Humor—when the instructor made a joke or a humorous comment

- Personal content—when the instructor inquired about the student's well-being or the well-being of the family or discussed other personal issues

The use of the native language in ESL or VESL instruction is also an issue that has surfaced as relevant to workforce education programs. Many instructors have expressed the need to use the native language in beginning-level classes, where the students have little or no proficiency in English. However, a switch to the native language is also appropriate in English language classes in other instances. Klaudia Rivera (1999a) writes that adult education programs whose aim is "to teach English language and literacy may use learners' native languages as instructional support in a variety of ways . . . for content area instruction, such as for health, immigration, or pre-employment preparation classes and counseling . . . to help students with basic vocabulary, concept-knowledge development, and semantic and syntactic understanding" (p. 2). In a discussion of a highly successful community education program which she conceived and directed, El Barrio Popular Education program in New York City, Rivera further elaborates on the significance of native language support in literacy development:

The use of the student's native language . . . [a]llowed for an education project that started from the known, the lived, the already experienced; it recognized and validated the strengths of the participants . . . language was used as a resource in the education of the students and as a main vehicle for the analysis and transformation of their reality. (Rivera, 1999b, p. 336)

Auerbach (1993) argues that the use of English only in ESL classes rests on unexamined assumptions and serves to reinforce social inequities. The use of English-only instruction, she explains, is rooted in practices in the early twentieth century that were designed to "Americanize" the population by promoting U.S. values. The use of English only was also a gate-keeping practice used to exclude qualified foreigners from the ranks of the teaching profession. With respect to current classroom practice, she states that "prohibiting the native language within the context of ESL instruction may impede language acquisition precisely because it mirrors disempowering relations" (p. 16). She adds that the use of English only also runs the danger of equating English with literacy skills, thus disregarding proficiencies in the native language and resulting in the improper placement of students.

The use of the native language in the ESL classroom can be a tool for reducing the affective barriers in the classroom, as confirmed by bilingual instructors who switch languages for humor or for establishing rapport. It can also promote the participation of adult students in dialogue centering around content that is at their cognitive level—that is, it does not reduce them to childlike uses of the language. Other uses for Spanish in English language classes with Latinos are suggested by Piasecka (cited in Auerbach, 1990). These include classroom management, scene-setting, language analysis, discussion of crosscultural issues, presentation of language rules, and assessment of comprehension. These uses do not promote the nondiscriminate use of the native language in the ESL or VESL class. They do, however, target the use of the native language for useful purposes, a practice that is confirmed by research in the area of language alternation in instruction.

In brief, even though instructors who use both languages intuitively cannot always articulate when or why they switch languages in the classroom, it appears that the switch from one language to another can play a strategic role in adult bilingual instruction. Research in bilingual instruction in workforce education programs is only now evolving, yet the findings from previous studies discussed above provide some guidelines for the use of Spanish and English that can be applied to bilingual instruction for adults. Application of language distribution strategies, however, demands expertise on the part of the teaching staff.

PROFESSIONAL DEVELOPMENT

The single most critical issue in the implementation of successful adult education programs is that of professional development. It is absolutely essential to hire qualified staff members who are bilingual, biliterate, and bicultural, and who have a conceptual foundation in the areas of second-language acquisition and literacy development as well as experience and a sense of caring, to teach a designated program component. Ongoing professional development for all teaching staff is missing from many programs that, at best, provide only an intensive one- or two-day training session for staff members when they come on board and/or attend workshops that are presented sporadically throughout the year. This piecemeal approach is ineffective, for as Knowlen (cited in Daley, 2000) says, "We know that many professionals attend CPE [continued professional education] only to shelve the large handouts and course materials they receive, never to look at them again" (p. 33). The implementation of professional development is complicated by the fact that the great majority of instructors are hired on a part-time basis. Burt and Keenan (1998) add that, like their students, these instructors "frequently have busy lives and find it hard to pursue additional training or education. Unlike most k-12 educators, teaching is often not their only or even their main job. In fact, 90 percent work part-time, are paid on an hourly basis, and do not receive benefits" (p. 4). Yet, continuous professional development must also be an integral part of all adult education programs, for it is only through ongoing sharing, learning, and dialoguing about issues and problems that instructors and other staff can grow professionally and can develop and implement solutions that ultimately will bring about student success.

An analysis of the quality of instruction that is offered in the ESL or VESL component of programs reveals that it is an area where the need for professional development appears to be most critically needed. English-language instruction is poor in many programs, particularly those that mostly hire part-time instructors whose only qualifications are that they are native speakers of English and have completed some college work. A recent study that focused on ESL classes for adults in workforce education programs found, for instance, that instructors generally focused on teaching "discrete, decontextualized, generic sets of skills" rather than on holistic, communicative uses of language relevant to the students' lives outside of the classroom (Calderon, 1999). Common student complaints about the classes were that there was too much grammar, not enough English was spoken, there was much wasted time in the classroom, a lack of teacher preparation, a lack of a sequential curriculum, and excessive use of Spanish in the classroom.

ESL instructors often lack a knowledge base with respect to second-language acquisition, literacy and biliteracy development, and adult-learning theory. Many are still entrenched within a structural framework of language teaching that revolves around grammar, one that is reinforced by the purchase by program administrators of textbooks that also present a structurally based curriculum rather than one based on an approach that focuses on communication (see chapter 4). This misguided, although well-intentioned, belief among many ESL instructors was expressed by one of the more experienced staff members during a group interview on bilingual instruction that was co-facilitated by the author. The instructor exclaimed that "students must learn grammar to learn English . . . and they must learn phonics!" He continued by explaining that he started beginners with the verb "be," then continued teaching the various verb tenses, and worked his way up to the construction of a sentence. A group of instructors at a different school revealed a lack of knowledge of basic learning theory that emphasizes the importance of recognizing and building on background knowledge and experiences that students bring with them to the classroom. These instructors continually emphasized how little these workers (some with thirty years of job experience!) knew and how they would almost have to "start from scratch" and "change their brains."

Despite the strong work ethic and many decades of faithful, uninterrupted service that many displaced workers have provided to former employers, some instructors still seemed to think that these students needed to be "taught discipline," rather than discussing, for instance, how they could help these workers transfer or adapt their self-discipline to the world of intensive study. Nonetheless, the sense of caring for their students was present among those instructors who participated in informal interviews, and who expressed that they would often tutor students on their own time in order to help them succeed. The concern for their students was also evident as instructors discussed their many efforts to motivate students and raise their self-esteem so that they would learn and reach their personal goals. One instructor, for instance, stated "I want to capture their hearts so that they want to do that!"

Nonetheless, it is difficult for many ESL instructors to break away from traditional paradigms that emphasize outdated methods of second-language teaching, particularly when they are not provided with ongoing professional development. The complexity of adult education for Latinos who come with diverse levels of bilingualism, native-language literacy, and formal schooling, and who face unemployment, poverty, and a myriad other challenges outside the classroom makes professional development for instructors an absolute mandate rather than an option. Adult-education instructors need to develop their conceptual knowledge in the area of curriculum and instruction for linguistically and culturally diverse groups, and they need to be proficient in the use of different instructional tools.

States have not developed credentialing requirements for instructors of adults as they have for instructors in public schools. The lack of a credentialing system has increasingly become the focus of attention over the past several years, however, and some states (such as Texas and Massachusetts) have begun to pilot programs for the credentialing of ABE and ESL instructors. Kutner (1992) identifies several formats for professional development, including conferences, workshops, summer institutes, university course-work, peer-coaching, and self-directed learning. Whatever the format, however, he adds that there are certain key elements to effective professional development. These are as follows:

- Conducting needs assessments that include state and local directors, instructors, and learners

- Involving teachings and volunteer instructors in the planning of training activities

- Creating a professional environment where instructors are compensated for engaging in development activities, recognized for their achievements, and respected as professionals

- Actively involving instructors in their own learning through, for example, peer-coaching and classroom research

In order for professional development to be implemented successfully, however, hiring practices must be reversed so that most instructors are full-time and not part-time. A full-time teaching staff will have increased time, dedication, and motivation for participating in professional development. Students will benefit from a full-time, professionally trained staff—they will achieve higher levels of learning, institutions and organizations will benefit by increased program success, and all of society will benefit from having a more educated citizenry.

There is, however, a political issue that has a significant impact on the ability of educators to carry out their jobs as professionals and that must be addressed if workforce education is to be effective. This issue is that instructors must be allowed to exercise their abilities as professionals. Yet, the entangled system of funding streams, eligibility criteria, work-first philosophy, and other agency requirements that are set by federally subsidized programs have limited the abilities of practitioners to exercise their professional beliefs about appropriate curriculum and instruction for the diverse groups of adult learners that they teach (see chapter 2). In the past, educators could use their professional judgement to determine the best methods for serving students who sought a better education. That power has been severely limited by the WIA and related legislation. Wilson (2000) elaborates on this loss, which has occurred not only among educators but among other professionals as well: "That power, traditionally the reserve of individual professionals and a function of individual discretionary judgment, is now rapidly being colonized by the systems in which individual professionals participate; it is now the systems, not individual professionals, who decide what clients need and how they will be served" (p. 75).

The bureaucratic system of adult education has furthermore depersonalized instruction and objectified individuals, who are not seen as human beings yet who have contributed immensely to society through their labor, citizenship, and belief in honest work, and who bring individual needs, strengths, and weaknesses to their desire for a better life. Rather, they are now seen as faceless groups with an array of problems, who are increasingly dependent on government for their welfare. The workforce education system that has been put in place through recent legislation is reminiscent of what Giddens (cited in Wilson, 2000) calls "expert systems," where services are delivered systematically and are based on a factory model rather than being delivered by practitioners working autonomously within the community. Thus, again, the notion of individual professional competency is being eroded.

This issue demands attention from all parties—educators, industry, and policymakers. While educators are not expected to function totally autonomously in our increasingly complex and global world, they should be provided with the freedom to exercise their professional judgements about how best to develop biliteracy, numeracy, critical thinking and other demand-skills for their adult students who are displaced and/or unemployed. This freedom, along with input from learners about their goals and interests, and from industry about occupational needs and requirements, will allow the development of educational programs that are pedagogically sound and that meet the needs and interests of all who are involved. This collaboration, however, must first respect the expertise of educators as professionals.

CHARACTERISTICS OF PROMISING BILINGUAL WORFORCE EDUCATION PROGRAMS

There is no single workforce education model that works for all groups. However, the research literature and existing programs have provided us with some insights about the characteristics of promising models for Latinos. Programs that are aimed at Latino Spanish-speaking populations must integrate and apply knowledge from the field of bilingual education if they are to be successful. Those programs that are experiencing success with Latinos who have low levels of formal education and little or no English-language proficiency share the following characteristics:

- Bilingual and biliterate administrative and instructional staff—This permits comfortable communication with students of diverse linguistic abilities and classroom instruction that is comprehensible to all students.

- Bilingual instructional materials—A choice of materials in English or Spanish meets the needs of learners who are dominant in one language or the other and provides the student with the opportunity to acquire more quickly the knowledge and competencies necessary to acquire the necessary credentials.

- A nurturing, caring, and motivational environment—Low self-esteem is common among unemployed workers. Success in a program requires a concerted and genuine effort among all staff to raise a student's motivation and self-esteem, and to tutor or do whatever is necessary to ensure that every student completes the program. Bicultural as well as bilingual staff are the keys to providing a nonthreatening, caring, familial, and empathetic environment where students can thrive.

- Instructional staff who are experienced and knowledgeable in the areas they are teaching—Expertise in a given area allows instructors to provide hands-on experiences and to adapt and implement other learning activities as appropriate.

- An integrated (rather than sequential) model that includes ESL or VESL, basic education, occupational training, and/or GED instruction—An integrated model allows students to progress more quickly through the occupational skills training and permits development and reinforcement of language and content across the different program components.

- Counseling and referrals to social service agencies for students facing educational barriers—Matching student skills and interests to the local job markets is crucial for successful, long-term employment. Assistance with childcare, transportation, and other possible barriers greatly raise a student's probability of completing a program.

- Close relationships and collaborations with industry—Collaborations with industry by way of curriculum development, internships, on-the-job training and field trips greatly enhance a student's probability of obtaining a job upon completion of a program. They provide an opportunity for both student and employer to become acquainted with each other and ensure a good match upon program completion.

- Employment placement assistance—Educators and students must both be knowledgeable about local job markets so that educators can provide the appropriate training and education. Job search assistance both during and upon completion of training is essential for placement in jobs that pay sustainable wages.

- Accountability—A successful program requires formative evaluations in order to track student progress toward achievement of their program goals as well as to satisfy accountability requirements set by funding agencies (see chapter 5 for a discussion of accountability and assessment). Ongoing student assessment so that students, instructors, and program administrators can monitor the learning that is taking place is also characteristic of successful programs. A variety of instruments can be used for accountability and assessment.

- Professional development—Staff development must be offered on an ongoing basis for high-quality instruction. This is particularly crucial for bilingual instruction. The teaching staff needs to familiarize itself with language distribution issues in the classroom as well as with other linguistic and cultural issues relevant to instruction.

The quality of classroom instruction, as discussed above, is one of the crucial elements involved in successful programs. There is no single teaching method that guarantees student learning for all groups. However, the research literature has provided us with pedagogical principles and practices that have resulted in higher levels of learning in diverse classrooms.

NOTE

1. At the time of this writing, the institution was making a transition to a change where only ESL and GED would be integrated for the first six months of study, the occupational area to be added beginning in the seventh month or upon reaching a level 2 of English proficiency (about sixth-grade level). However, the program integrated all three components during its first ten months of operation.

Graduation ceremony for newly licensed students. Photograph by author.

Group work in a vocational ESL class. Photograph by author.

Spanish GED class. Photograph by author.

Bilingual medical assistant vocational class. Photograph by author.

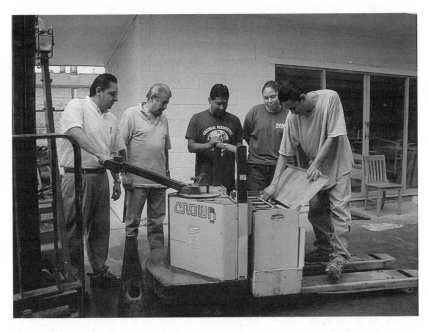

Instructor assisting students in a bilingual warehousing and shipping class. Photograph by author.

Clients going through intake at a one-stop center. Photograph by author.

Student presentation in a bilingual plastic injection molding class. Photograph by author.

Painting created in protest of NAFTA by adult bilingual learners. Photograph by author.

Painting created by adult bilingual students in a literacy class. Photograph by author.

Students working with a plastic injection molding machine. Photograph by author.

Student learning to word process shipping forms. Photograph by author.

Instructor tutoring student. Photograph by author.

4

PRINCIPLES AND
PRACTICES IN EDUCATING
THE LATINO WORKFORCE

The quality of the curriculum and instruction in workforce education programs is critical to their success. There is no single blueprint for what curriculum and instruction should look like, for there are multiple factors to be
considered. In designing a curriculum, for instance, one must consider the
goals of the learners and of the specific program they are enrolled in, and
the expectations of prospective employers. The levels of education, of language proficiencies, and the background knowledge that students bring
with them to a classroom are also determining factors in curriculum design.
There are no definitive methods or instructional practices guaranteed to
bring about success, for the methodologies that are used are relative to the
learners and their background, to the curricular tasks at hand, and to available resources and time, and so forth. Central to curriculum and instruction
is the notion of literacy itself. What does it mean to be literate, and does this
change in diverse contexts? What are the expectations that employers have
of employees in terms of literacy? What are the realities of the workplace
with respect to the literacy demands of the job? Contrary to traditional notions of literacy, the concept of literacy and of workplace literacy, specifically, is dynamic and multidimensional.

A RECONCEPTUALIZATION OF WORKPLACE LITERACY

Traditional models of literacy instruction focused on a grammar-based
curriculum that was centered on the reading and writing of texts. These

texts often consisted of contrived passages whose content was irrelevant to the learner but which were structurally designed to meet different levels of grammatical complexity for students with diverse levels of language proficiencies. Instruction was very didactic and often took the form of fill-in-the-blanks, matching pictures to words, matching columns of vocabulary, and grammatical analysis of sentences.

The SCANS competencies that were issued in 1991 brought about a change in teaching methodology from the traditional, didactic, decontextualized form of instruction to a more integrated form of instruction, which emphasized academic and occupational knowledge as applied to the workplace. As a result of SCANS, therefore, one finds an emphasis on what has been called "functional context" in workplace literacy and education programs. In an effort to make the content less abstract, learning is placed within real work environments so that students apply what they have learned to a work context. Activities in literacy development, for instance, might involve reading a company bulletin or newspaper, writing a memo to a supervisor, filling in charts indicating the quantities of work orders processed, reading the directions in a manual that accompanies a piece of machinery, or reading a poster on occupational safety requirements. Schultz (1992) argues against this competency model of education, which assumes that literacy, and particularly workplace literacy, is "a set of universal skills disassociated from the individual and made specific by the functional context in which they are applied" (p.11). She advocates for a perspective that emphasizes the essentially social nature of literacy and that focuses not only on the tasks of the workplace but also on understanding the social and political relations that surround work and the possibilities for transforming both the workplace and one's position within it.

Workplace education programs, however, have instead focused on developing curricula for specific vocational areas using task analysis. This involves the instructor or appropriate individual going into a workplace, observing and interviewing workers, and analyzing the performance requirements of the jobs in question in order to come up with a discrete list of "skill requirements," which are then taught to the participants in the program. For example, part of the curriculum for an occupational-specific course on plastic injection molding might require that the students be able to label all the major parts of a molding machine and explain each of its major functions, be able to operate the molding machine, recognize defective parts, and know the do's and don'ts with respect to occupational safety.

Innovative approaches to literacy development go beyond lists of discrete skills and beyond the isolated skills of reading, writing, and memorizing to include all forms of communication, including oral language and telecommunications. Whole texts whose content is relevant and interesting to the learners, such as authentic trade literature, brochures, subject-matter books (social studies, science), and personal diaries or journals, are used to develop literacy. Pedogogical activities include dialogue, creative writing, community or class-based projects, and the use of technology as a tool for problem-solving, publishing, and communication. Along with this has come a reconceptualization of literacy or "literacies" as culturally based practices that can be understood only within given social contexts. Literacies, for example, might include the ability to read the Koran in an Arabic culture or the ability to tell stories and carry on other forms of oral traditions of Mexican and other Latino cultures. Within a given culture, academic literacy differs from literacy as it is used in everyday life, and both of these literacies differ from workplace literacies as they occur within given work sites. An example of the latter is an analytical study (Hart-Landsberg and Reder, 1997) of a factory that manufactures automobile accessories, which presented different literacy issues than did a study of a computer-manufacturing plant (Darrah, 1997).

The acquisition of literacy, moreover, is not only viewed as a sociocultural practice, but is also seen, from a critical perspective, as empowering learners to take an active role in their learning and to effect positive change in their worlds. Spener (1993) writes that literacy "helps provide people with the tools to intervene actively in the shaping and transformation of their social reality by deepening their knowledge of that reality" (p. 77). Fingeret (cited in Schultz, 1992) adds to this by emphasizing the political nature of literacy. "Literacy is not some naturally occurring object. . . . It is a social construct—it is defined and created by those in power in a society, and those definitions change as conditions change. Thus, literacy is considered historically and culturally relative; definitions of literacy depend on time and place (although they are always decided upon by those in positions of power" (p. 13).

The author is thus suggesting that what is known as functional literacy, or in this case literacy within a workplace context, is defined by those in power—in other words, employers, supervisors, and other management. Literacy is multilayered in that it requires an understanding of the social context in which it takes place. In the workplace, this translates into an understanding of the cultural, political, and economic realities of a specific work situation. This presents a much more complex notion of workplace literacy requirements than can be carried out by the typical task analysis or job audit as performed by curriculum developers or other outsiders. The research literature provides examples of how employees have actually used literacy in its more complex forms at various work sites.

Baba (1991) reports on ethnographic studies of work activities as they were performed at a variety of industrial work sites. One of the findings was that the occupational skills studied almost always required informal collective action among individuals. An observation of an automated manufacturing-plant start-up revealed that work groups and their supervisors gathered together informally each day before the start of the first shift (at 5

A.M.) to review the day's objectives and discuss any anticipated problems. An ethnography of construction workers found that independent groups of craftsmen voluntarily agreed to arrive at the work site before dawn in order to pour twice as much concrete as scheduled. Another study by an anthropologist at a Xerox plant involved the repair of a complex new model of copier. Because the model was new, the company was unable to provide the technicians with exhaustive formal training or documentation on the problems with it that might be encountered. The researcher found that repair technicians used communally shared narratives (machine repair "war stories" or anecdotes) as models in the diagnosis and testing of the equipment systems. The narratives provided information on the machine as well as on the specific use situation. A "communal memory" was thus established over time. These mental models aided in the organization of new knowledge and served as a frameworks for the retrieval of information. The author notes that management was often unaware of the strategies implemented in such work performance and that the skills used were not often reflected on the job descriptions nor related by the workers when asked about what their various jobs entailed. Baba writes: "Work performance often involves specialized forms of know-how . . . that are developed by workers in order to enhance work output, but are unknown or unrecognized by management" (p. 4). In essence, all of the workers used literacy in more complex ways than just implementing isolated tasks.

Darrah's (1997) in-depth look into the skill requirements of workers at a computer-assembly plant confirmed these findings. The study revealed that the assembly tasks were neither simple, linear, nor predictable as described by the management, engineers, and production workers. Observations, for instance, revealed that interruptions on the assembly line were the rule and not the exception. Workers often returned to work on units because needed parts were often missing and arrived hours or days later. System-repair technicians were also required to work on several simultaneous units at once and explained that it was a challenge to "systematically and simultaneously juggle swapping in several units while the automated tests cycled through their sequences" (p. 257). Descriptive and prescriptive writing was also required—in very clear and specific ways—in the "shift passdown notes" which workers leaving one shift left for the incoming shift. The reorganization of the workplace at the plant into teams necessitated additional social, political, and economic skills that were complex.

These analyses of work activities raise several issues beyond the scope of this book, such as the lack of participatory management processes at the workplace, and the lack of understanding by management about the types of knowledge required for the workers to perform their tasks more efficiently and successfully interact with other personnel. The principal issue as relevant to literacy development is that workplace requirements are generally more complex than what might be described through task analysis or any type of job audit. The job situation required that workers have a broad understanding of their jobs in terms of communication, politics, and economics, as well as other more discrete skills such as numeracy, dexterity, and organization. The notion of task analysis in developing workplace literacy curricula can greatly simplify work activity and, in fact, serve to blame workers for substandard work performance when in reality the problem lies elsewhere.

INSTRUCTION FOR THE LATINO WORKFORCE

The studies described above have significant implications in the case of Latino and other minority workers, who are often described as lacking the literacy skills needed for better-paying positions. Curricula and instruction must go beyond a concrete list of skills accumulated through job audits, and beyond rote memorization and labeling of parts of machinery or other equipment. This presents a major challenge to instructors and learners, particularly when the learners come into a class with very low levels of formal schooling, as is the case with the U.S.–Mexico Borderland populations. Thus, a first critical step that curriculum developers, instructors, and other educators involved in workforce education must take is to achieve a conceptual understanding of how adults learn and how literacies are acquired. While there is no definitive list of what successful instructors must know or be able to do, the field has provided some principles of adult learning that can inform practitioners and that are particularly applicable to working with unemployed and/or displaced Latinos.

Affective Factors

The affective aspects of learning are most significant for those students with low levels of prior schooling. It is critical that the instructor create a classroom learning environment that is warm, caring, and nurturing for the student. Brown (1994) writes that language learners feel fragile and inhibited when they "must fend for their emotional selves with a paltry linguistic battery that leaves them with a feeling of total defenselessness" (p. 22). Workers are threatened by the idea of returning to school after decades of not being in a classroom. Their low levels of schooling and negative classroom experiences in the past compound the anxiety they feel upon returning to school. This is particularly true for Latinos, many of whom received what little formal education they have in Mexico, where the system of education is markedly different from that of the United States. It is imperative that the instructors demonstrate a sincere interest in the well-being of each student and that they be willing to listen to students and refer them for assistance, as appropriate, when obstacles arise. Some ways to demonstrate caring are to greet students by name, to inquire about their well-being and that of their family, to praise individual and group accomplishments in the class, and to take time to periodically confer individually with students regarding class progress and related issues. A cautionary note is that creating a nurturing environment does not imply that the role of the teacher changes to that of a parent, nor that teachers should allow students to be complacent instead of pushing them to learn and to excel. As Freire (1998) says in his discussion of the ideologies inherent in the roles of teachers and parents, "Being a teacher implies the responsibility to assume the demands of a profession. . . . Accepting the reduction of teaching to mere parenting . . . takes away certain professional responsibilities of the teacher" (p. 4). Thus, as professionals, instructors must find a balance between being nurturing and exercising their duties to teach and help students attain their educational goals. Students must be held up to high educational standards, and instructors must assist them in meeting those standards.

The development of student motivation and self-confidence upon entry into the classroom is another issue. Adult students, particularly those who have been unemployed, displaced, and/or on Temporary Assistance to Needy Families (TANF) for some time tend to have low self-confidence. Their self-confidence must be raised if they are going to be successful in an education program. Instructors can assist with this by presenting Latino role models to the class who also struggled greatly with their education; by bringing past "graduates" into the class who are now successfully working; by implementing specific techniques that are designed to raise motivation levels such as repetition of positive phrases throughout the day, or by having students relate personal accomplishments such as raising a family; and by periodically having students reflect and write about their progress toward their short-term goals.

Student-learning diaries are particularly useful in helping students reflect on progress toward their educational goals, on day-to-day accomplishments, and on their learning strengths and weaknesses. These diaries may be filled out in Spanish and/or English. The intent is to periodically engage the student in self-reflection and self-direction using the language(s) that are most comfortable for him or her, and also to provide useful information for the instructor regarding the success and direction of classroom instruction. If a student indicates, for instance, that he or she had problems with a particular area, then the instructor can repeat that lesson or present it again using an alternative approach. It is always easier for a student to communicate a lack of understanding privately, as in a learner diary, rather than publicly in class. Learner diaries may be filled out once a week or more frequently, as deemed appropriate by the instructor and students. A sample ESL learner diary is seen in Figure 4.1.

Participatory Classrooms

Participatory classrooms, where the lived experiences and cultural and linguistic knowledge that students bring with them to the classroom is val-

Figure 4.1
Learner Diary

Two things that I learned this week are
One thing that was not clear to me was
This week I spoke English to
This week I read
One thing that I want to learn is
By next week I will be able to

ued, are essential. Integrating student experiences, knowledge, and opinions into classroom discussions, for instance, not only raises student motivation and self-esteem but also provides a bridge for instructors to learn more about their students. This connection to the lives of students outside of the classroom allows for the development of learning activities that are relevant and applicable to students' lives. Auerbach (1996) states that the participatory model for adult ESL literacy "offers a systematic process for building curriculum around learners' lived experiences and social realities" (p. 11). This is particularly essential in working with Latinos who, although they share a common language, come from many countries with diverse backgrounds and cultures. Research, moreover, has indicated that students learn when instructors engage the initial understandings of students when teaching new concepts or information—that is, when they use the students' background knowledge and experiences as a springboard for teaching new concepts (National Research Council, 2000). In the case of language learning, it is imperative that instructors build upon the literacy skills that learners bring with them in Spanish in order to facilitate the transfer to English.

This applies to the cultural aspects of learning as well. Research has indicated that learning is a sociocultural process that begins at the time we are born as we interact with other members of our group. Trueba (1990) writes, "Language and culture are inseparable in the process of mediation between social and mental processes that constitute the instructional process. . . . Language and culture play a key role in the organization of cognitive tasks, the development of critical thinking skills, and the process of creative thinking" (pp. 2–3). This research is highly relevant to education with Latinos, for it implies that classrooms must provide a social context for learning that allows them to access knowledge in ways that are comfortable for them. It is imperative, for instance, that instructors integrate participation formats into their classrooms that include modeling and collaborative work, both of which are characteristic of learning processes in Latino cultures.

Because group collaboration rather than individual competition is emphasized in Latino cultures, for example, the instructor of a course on childcare might regularly integrate group assignments into the class as a participation format. Such an assignment might be to design a healthy snack and lunch menu for a week for a home day-care center that has an enrollment of eight toddlers. Rather than assign this individually, the instructor would divide the class into small groups of three to five people and would have each group come up with a single menu and a rationale for the food selections included in the menu. A series of tasks (for example, aligning meals with the food pyramid, determining nutritional content, determining portions, recipe selection, etc.) would be provided for each group in order to help them distribute the work load and to ensure that each member of the group would be contributing to the assignment. This type of collaborative work assignment would not only be more familiar and comfortable for the students, but would also be pedagogically sound because it would allow for interpersonal communication, the discussion of diverse ideas and viewpoints, and the development of negotiation skills among the students.

As mentioned earlier, the oral tradition is strong in Latino cultures and is often practiced through storytelling in the form of "cuentos" [short folktales handed down orally through the generations]. Another example of cultural integration into the curriculum would be for the instructor to focus not just on storybook reading but also on the use of "cuentos" as part of the literacy-building activities that are appropriate for children of all ages. This discussion might be started by asking the students to share some of the stories that were told to them by their grandparents or parents as they were growing up.

A popular tool among instructors that facilitates the integration of student cultural, linguistic, or factual background knowledge into the teaching and learning process is the KWL (Know, Want to Know, Learned) chart. An even more useful tool, however, is the KWLH chart (see figure 4.2). The addition of the H (How I Will Learn) develops the self-directed learning process in students by having them reflect on how they will learn something new that is of interest to them. It prepares them for the twenty-first-century world where what counts is not necessarily what you know, but more importantly, if you know how to access needed information.

The first two columns of the KWLH chart are filled out at the beginning of a new lesson or unit. The teacher begins by posing open-ended questions that are relevant to the new information to be presented in class in order to encourage students to share what they already know that is related to the upcoming lesson(s). For a lesson on organizing a budget, for example, the instructor might pose the following questions for discussion:

- Have you ever wanted to buy something but decided not to? Why not?
- What things did you think about when making your decision?

Figure 4.2
KWLH Chart

Know	Want to Know	Learned	How Will Learn More

- Can you always buy the things that you want to buy?
- Have you worked on any projects that required the purchase of materials? How did you decide whether or not to purchase those materials?
- What other things do you spend money on?
- What types of things do you not spend your money on? Why?

After students have shared their responses to the questions, the class is ready to fill out the first column of the chart—"Know." In this column, the teacher lists some of the things that the students already know about budgeting, that surfaced during the discussion. A student, for instance, might share that she purchased cake-decorating materials and occasionally takes orders for cakes, makes and decorates the cakes at home, and sells them for a given price. Others might share that they try to save money for food and electricity before they purchase other things. From this, the instructor would list things under the Know column of the chart such as "some purchases are more important than others," "a limited amount of money often has to cover many expenses," or "think carefully about overall expenses before spending money." Follow-up questions would then be asked regarding what students would like to know about spending/not spending money, such as strategies for determining "best buys." This information would be entered in the second column under "Want to Know." The concept of a budget would then be introduced. Students might be presented with sample budgets and guided in coming up with lists of their own monthly expenses. Ideas would be presented on how to save money, how to plan ahead, how to find the lowest price for similar items, and so forth. After a series of learning activities related to budgeting, the class would collaboratively fill out the third column, "Learned." Here they would list some of the things learned during the lesson(s). Finally, they would brainstorm on sources of information for finding out more about budgeting. This might include anything from talking to relatives about how they manage their budgets, to reading magazines and brochures, to consulting a financial officer at a credit union. This information would be filled out in the last column, "How to Learn More." The appropriate follow-up activities would then be implemented, from which students would come up with additional ideas on budgeting.

Hands-On Experiences

Hands-on experiences are essential in both the academic and the occupational classroom. In the case of English language development, this translates to the implementation of authentic communicative activities in the classroom, as opposed to having didactic exercises where students, for instance, conjugate verbs or fill in the blanks on ditto sheets. Classrooms that integrate authentic communicative activities are highly interactive and emphasize the meaning, or content, of language rather than its structure. Students (including those at the beginning levels), for example, engage in dialogue, role-play, reading of authentic literature such as short stories and poems, and self-expressive writing as appropriate for their level of proficiency. This communicative approach is confirmed by Richard-Amato (1996), who states that "meaningful interaction seems to be the key" (p. 41) to language learning. She elaborates by citing the research of theorists such as Vygotsky and Bruner, who emphasized the social nature of learning and of the acquisition of language. Heath (1989), in her anthropological research on child-rearing and learning practices across diverse cultures, confirms the importance of learning through observation and by doing in the Mexican culture. Mexican children learn by taking on specific tasks of varying complexity, as they are deemed ready by the parents. She writes, "Modeling and close observation, supplemented by reinforcement through praise or caution, surround the teaching of most tasks in the home" (p. 173). Torres-Guzmán et al. (1994), in their studies of working with diverse populations, also emphasize the significance of learning through doing rather than through verbal explanations in Latino cultures.

Hands-on experiences are also critical for effective learning in the occupational classroom. An occupation, additionally, is best learned when the experiences are provided by someone who has had years of work experience in the particular area being taught. Wrigley (personal communication, November 10, 2000) has found in her research that the most promising approaches to workforce development include spending considerable time on hands-on activities provided by experienced occupational instructors, a notion that has also been confirmed by the Center for Employment Training (CET) and other successful programs that have a long history of providing education for the workforce.

A VESL lesson, for example, might focus on job benefits. A hands-on assignment would be for the students to find out new information about the types of benefits provided by different local companies and to practice previously learned grammatical structures and words used for questions in English, such as "Do you . . . ?" and "Does your company . . . ?" In addition to developing a discussion on the different types of benefits offered by American companies and what the benefits cover, the instructor might also have two students model a previously prepared role-play in which one student is a potential employee and the other is a personnel clerk with a prospective employer. The potential employee then develops a dialogue with the clerk, posing questions about the benefits offered by the company, such as:

- "Do you offer medical insurance?"
- "What about dental insurance?"
- "Do you get paid sick days?"

This dialogue could be practiced with several groups of students, the instructor providing an opportunity for the students to vary the questions and responses a bit from the original script each time. The dialogue could, for instance, take place between two close friends or neighbors, where one is inquiring about the other's job benefits. This hands-on experience would then be followed by an assignment where the learning activity would be applied in the "real world" outside of the classroom. The instructor would ask the students to actually meet with an English-speaking friend or relative who is working full-time. The assignment would be to conduct a mini-interview: the student would ask the friend the name of the company that he or she works for and the types of benefits that are provided by that company. The information would be brought back to class and shared with the rest of the students. Together, they would have a pool of new information about the types of benefits offered by different companies in the area. Hands-on experiences are appropriate across the various curricular components of a workforce education program. A hands-on experience for a GED math class studying areas of different shapes would be to go home and figure out the total wall area for two rooms in their home that were to be painted. They could then apply this to a problem in which they had to figure out how many quarts of paint they would need, assuming that each quart covered a given number of square feet.

Hands-on experiences are typically more common in occupational classes, where the students actually work with equipment, drive a truck, enter data into a computer, and so forth. When these classes comprise one component of a workforce education program, it is important that literacy development also be integrated into the class. This can be done in English and/or Spanish, as appropriate. An assignment, for instance, might be for the students to learn the names of the different parts of a molding machine. The instructor would review the names of each part and their function using a large diagram or picture of the machine, with each part explicitly labeled. A hands-on experience would follow. The students would be grouped in pairs and sent into the lab. There, they would examine the molding machine, identify each of the parts, and observe the movement and function of each part as the machine was in operation. Each student would "teach" the other student about the machine as he or she named, identified, and explained the function of each part to the other student. A follow-up in-class assignment would be for the students to write a paragraph regarding their observations in the lab and/or write a list of the parts of the machine with a sentence describing the function of each part. Additionally, each pair of students might be asked to formulate a question about the machine. These questions would be written on flip charts or on a chalkboard. They would then be read by the class. Students who could respond to given questions would circulate around the room writing the responses to the various questions posted on either the flip chart or the board. The instructor would assist with those questions that the students could not answer. The written questions and responses would be reviewed once more by the class as a whole.

This activity would most probably be done in English, as the students would need to be able to refer to manuals and memos on the machine written in English once they were at the workplace. However, a follow-up lesson on troubleshooting a machine that was not functioning appropriately might be conducted bilingually or in Spanish. The use of the stronger language would facilitate comprehension of complex explanations regarding the possible malfunctioning of various parts of the machine and the solutions for fixing the problem. Names for specific malfunctions, however, could be additionally reviewed in English, particularly if they were names or processes commonly identified in the manuals that accompany the machine.

Multilevel Teaching

Despite the use of placement exams, all classes will have some diversity with respect to the academic and language proficiencies of the students. Multilevel teaching is essential in order to provide instruction that is comprehensible yet challenging to students, for one size does not fit all in terms of instruction. Multilevel teaching demands a high level of knowledge and expertise on the part of instructors. They must design learning activities that are flexible and open-ended, and that will facilitate learning on the part of the students, so that they are always progressing towards their academic and career goals. This most often requires that the instructor modify the textbook or other existing curriculum in order to accommodate, yet challenge, a given group of students. The ESL class is often the most diverse in terms of language proficiency. Following are some examples of learning activities that are open-ended in terms of the complexity of the responses required by the students.

The functions of language (for example, apologizing, requesting directions, asking for clarification, etc.) can be taught so that they allow students to respond at levels that are appropriate for them. A dialogue in which the student is requesting directions to the personnel office, for instance, can be modeled in varying formats, all of which communicate the same ideas or inquiries. Beginning students might ask, "Where is the personnel office?" Intermediate-level students might say, "Excuse me, I'm new here and I'm looking for the personnel office." An advanced student might use this format: "Excuse me, I need a job application. I wonder if you could tell me where the personnel office is located?"

The use of photos, magazine cutouts, posters, or collages can be used as catalysts for language use at different levels. As a response to a given photograph, for instance, students can either (a) name the item in the picture, (b) write a phrase(s) describing the picture, (c) write a sentence that describes the picture, (d) write a paragraph about the picture or about feelings elicited by the picture, or (e) write a story to accompany the picture. The same can be done with film clips, where students can describe scenes, answer questions about the characters, and/or respond to higher level questions about the clip ("Why do you think she said that?"), depending on the proficiency of the student.

Classroom demonstrations are ideal for multilevel teaching, as they provide a starting point for all students. The use of props and real objects that are brought into the classroom allows the students to do varying degrees of talking and explaining, while still providing a successful demonstration where students learn how to do something, as well as the specific vocabulary accompanied with that project or task. An ESL class, for instance, might ask pairs of students to present a classroom demonstration on a favorite hobby, such as candy-making or wood-carving. An occupational class for medical assistants might involve a demonstration of how to properly mount the EKG readings on the display board so that the doctor can examine them.

A GED class on literature and writing typically involves the analysis of short stories or excerpts from longer pieces of literature. Keating (1996) uses a technique that he calls the Heart of Reading. The technique consists of posing five simple questions that can elicit anything from simple single-phrase responses to a response consisting of a paragraph or more. The questions are designed to check student comprehension of the piece and also to develop critical thinking in students by calling on them to reflect on their interpretation of the story (or the big idea) and its application to their personal realities. The five questions are as follows:

- What happened at the beginning of the story?
- What happened in the middle of the story?
- What happened at the end of the story?
- What was the big idea in the story?
- What do you think about the story?

The questions are first discussed orally by the class. Sample responses are written on the board during the discussion. After the discussion, the students are then asked to write their individual responses to the questions. A beginning-level student in the ESL class might start out by simply copying one of the shorter responses that is modeled on the chalk board. A more advanced student might compose one, two, or three paragraphs in response to some of the questions.

Games are appropriate for the classroom, as long as they are relevant to the curriculum and carefully planned. They also serve to increase the motivation and engagement levels of the students. Games can be designed so that students with diverse abilities take on roles with differing demands. In a game that calls for the completion of a sentence, for instance, some students might come up with the missing words or phrases and call them out to another member of the team, who would simply write them down as dictated. In guessing games, some students might formulate the questions, while others simply respond with a one-word answer. Project-based learning consists of a series of interrelated learning activities that culminate in a project. This type of learning requires perhaps more careful planning and organization on the part of the instructor and students than do other types of activities—however, it is also most appropriate for multilevel teaching. A class, for example, might collaboratively decide to publish Family Journals as a project. This would involve students investigating their own family histories, interviewing family members, collecting photographs, labeling or describing photographs, and writing narratives about their families. The project would also involve some artwork in the designing of the covers, binding, and page layouts for their individual books.

This type of project could be successfully implemented in a class with diverse talents and abilities. The sharing of ideas and mutual assistance among students would facilitate the project for those students having more difficulties with the various activities. Still, students with lower literacy levels could simply write shorter narratives in their books and/or include an audiotape with additional information such as family anecdotes or stories. Those with higher literacy levels might include longer written narratives, such as descriptions and folktales. Project-based learning is as appropriate for the occupational classroom as for the GED or ESL classroom. Projects can also be implemented in the language(s) that is most appropriate—a GED class might opt to do the books in Spanish whereas an ESL class might do them bilingually or all in English. Project-based learning is equally effective across program components and can be implemented in English and/or Spanish.

Metacognitive Skills

Metacognitive skills (the ability to monitor our own levels of understanding) should also be integrated into the curriculum, particularly because many Latinos who enroll in workforce education programs have been out of school for years and because they face the additional challenge of having to learn another language. While they bring with them many lived experiences that have made them wiser and stronger individuals, they need to learn how to learn in the classroom. The integration of metacognitive skills (i.e., learning strategies) into the curriculum involves explicitly teaching students to reflect on their own learning processes and how they learn best. Learning strategies, for instance, might involve anything from working with a partner, to learning how to summarize or group ideas, to asking questions for clarification. Research into how people learn indicates that the "integration of metacognitive instruction with discipline based learning can enhance student achievement and . . . should be consciously incorporated into curricula across disciplines and age levels" (National Research Council, 2000, p. 21). The teaching of learning strategies is appropriate for all components of a workforce education program. Basic literacy, ESL, VESL, GED, or occupational classes, for instance, can all reinforce the development of these skills. They can also be taught in either or both languages. As is true of other knowledge and skills, the techniques that are learned will transfer to the alternate language when needed and can be applied across diverse contexts. A learning strategy that could be used in a GED math class, for example, would be to teach students to draw images that help them set up and solve problems. For a problem that required calculating the total perimeters of different shapes, the student could first draw the shapes and label the measurement of each side. He or she could then proceed to add or multiply the different measurements, as appropriate. A problem calling for fractions or ratios could also be solved by drawing figures, such as a pizza divided into equal slices. Students in another GED class that focuses on literature could be taught to use selective attention as a learning strategy. Before reading a passage, the student would skim through the comprehension questions at the end of the segment to get an idea of the types of information he would need to look for in the passage in order to answer the questions. During the reading process, the reader would pay particular attention when coming across the specific information called for in the questions. As another strategy, students could also be taught to highlight important information while they are reading.

A strategy that would help students monitor their own learning in an occupational class would be to teach them to make their own flash cards at home. Using the flash cards, they could practice and then "test" themselves on explaining the functions of different parts of a machine by, for example, writing the name of the part on one side and the function on the other side of the card. Cards could also be used in a class for medical assistants. On separate cards the student would write each of the steps for proper placement of EKG equipment on a patient. The student would then arrange the cards in the proper sequence, to reflect the correct implementation of the procedure.

Praxis in Workforce Education

The notion of "multiliteracies" as opposed to a single literacy implies that classroom practice in workforce education must be extended to learning activities that promote problem-solving skills and critical thinking as opposed to learning only reading, writing, and discrete skills related to a specific occupation. This calls for a fluid approach to the organization and discussion of the content of language and work-related study. Auerbach and Wallerstein (1987) presented one such approach, which has been successfully used across disciplines and with diverse learners of varying ages—"problem-posing." The problem-posing approach revolves around the discussion of issues drawn from the real-life experiences of the adult learners, followed by an action plan that is also developed through reflection and discussion by the learners in collaboration with the instructor. The plan of action focuses on ways to confront and/or solve issues that are of concern to the learners. In essence, this leads to what Doane (1998) has called a "praxis-spiral."

The praxis-spiral is transformative. Through this process learners begin with what they know, then "on reflection and exploration of generative themes, clarify what [they] need to lead to action" (p. 159). Graman (1988) describes this as the problematizing of reality: the classroom prepares students to critically analyze real problems and the significance of those problems on their own lives and the lives of others, and take action to solve them. He writes that "learning another language . . . can be a first step in gaining a critical consciousness of the interconnection among the lives of all people . . . to encounter and confront linguistic, cognitive, and axiological conflicts" (p. 442). In any case, what is essential is that instruction go beyond functional context skills as identified by job audits or task analyses and extend to the development of multiliteracies and critical thinking. These are potentially transformative, and will allow workers not only to obtain jobs with just treatment and sustainable wages but also to advance to better paying positions and eventually to pursue higher education.

Auerbach and Wallerstein (1987) present a curriculum that emphasizes the development of multiliteracies and critical thinking. One of the lessons in this curriculum, for instance, focuses on rules and responsibilities at the workplace. As part of this lesson, the students are asked to think about and discuss a list of rules and responsibilities for workers. Some of these rules are as follows:

- No talking on the job
- No reading on the job
- No music or radios on the job
- You must be on time for work
- No one else can punch in or out for you
- You must stay in your work area
- You may not take tools home

The students discuss what each rule means, which rules could be true for all jobs and which would apply to certain jobs only, the reason for the rules, and whether they think a rule is fair or unfair. This is followed by a presentation of various scenarios and dialogues between a worker and an employer involving a violation of rules. The students are asked to role-play a series of dialogues involving situations where, for example, they had car trouble on the way to work, they had a sick child and came in late, or they sprained their ankle at work. In the process, they are taught various ways to respond to discipline at work using apologies, explanations, and/or excuses. However, they are also taught—through vocabulary review, dialogues, and conversation—how to identify the responsibilities of the employer, how to respond to unfair discipline, and how to advocate for themselves by filing a grievance against an employer or asking for professional advice. The lesson includes a review of the National Labor Relations Act and information on the rights of workers to organize for change.

In the final part of the lesson, the students are called on to develop an action plan to be implemented outside of the classroom. There are options for this. One plan has students inquire about rules for employers and employees at specific local companies. They then design a chart that compares the rules and serves as a catalyst for discussion. The chart would include categories that would be filled in with information from the different companies. These categories could be (a) Employees have to . . . ; (b) Employees cannot . . . ; (c) Employers have to . . . ; and (d) Employers cannot. . . . Another possible action plan is to interview a friend or coworker about a situation at work that involved a problem with the rules. Questions they might pose during the interview are as follows:

- Have you ever tried to change anything with a group of coworkers?
- What was the problem?
- What did you do?
- What happened?

This lesson not only develops communicative skills but also develops those literacies and critical-thinking skills that enable a worker to advocate for himself or herself in the case of unjust treatment. This is crucial in workforce education, for as discussed in chapter 2, discriminatory practices against Latinos both on the job and during the recruiting process have been reported. This lesson, moreover, could be implemented by using only English or both English and Spanish, where Spanish would be used to discuss some of the more complex notions regarding workers' rights and processes. The use of Spanish in an ESL class, even beyond the beginning levels, may be not only appropriate but necessary, for as Auerbach (1993) states, the monolingual approach to ESL "denies learners the right to draw on their language resources and strengths; by forcing a focus on childlike uses of language and excluding the possibility of critical reflections, it may ultimately feed into the replication of relations of inequality outside the classroom" (p. 22).

Technology Integration

The integration of technology into the curriculum can facilitate student learning and highly increase motivation. Technology, however, should be used as a tool that will enhance student understanding and not as an end, or a skill, in and of itself. This is a particularly important point to remember because much of the software that is currently published is attractively put together (that is, with sound, motion, graphics) and it is easy for an instructor to let the students dwell on it for hours. However, even though some of this software is very attractive, it actually focuses on language as a discrete skill and often amounts to no more than a traditional skill-drill workbook that has been computerized. Technology should not drive the curriculum—the curriculum should drive the technology that is to be used. A simple word-processing program with tools such as a dictionary and thesaurus, for example, can greatly assist students to edit and publish their short stories, poems, compositions, or other narratives. Student autobiographies, short stories, or class newsletters can also be composed and easily illustrated using one of the many publishing programs available. Student survey data can be compiled and more easily analyzed using electronic spreadsheets, and software can likewise be used to create slide shows for student presentations. Digital cameras can facilitate publishing projects such as a neighborhood history booklet or a booklet on murals found in the community. Videotapes can also be used in a variety of ways in the classroom to develop English language proficiency. The instructor, for instance, can select brief segments of a movie and show them with the sound off so that students can compose the script, or a brief segment can be shown followed by an exercise in which students describe the scene and the action.

Technology can be particularly appropriate for Latinos and other linguistically diverse groups. The graphics, images, and sound can greatly enhance comprehension and analyses of subject matter by students acquiring English. The vast amounts of information available through the internet can additionally facilitate the development of the reasoning and critical-thinking skills through problem-solving exercises that are of real-world interest. Spanish language videos and software are also readily available and can also enrich the curriculum in an adult basic education, GED, or occupational class.

A unit that would integrate technology and develop critical-thinking skills, for instance, might involve the students in researching the response to a question such as "What percentage of small businesses in the United States are owned by Hispanics?" With guidance from the instructor, the students would search the appropriate databases and links on the internet, such as http://www.hispanic.com (*Hispanic Magazine* web site) and http://www.nclr.org (National Council of La Raza web site) to find relevant information. Related questions would then be generated, such as "What percentage are owned by Whites, Blacks, or Asians?" and "What percentage of the U.S. population do each of these groups represent?" The disproportionate ratios would then be discussed, to be followed by dialogue and further research on related issues, such as bank lending practices for small-business loans for Latinos. This lesson could culminate with the students inquiring at the Chamber of Commerce about the lending records of selected banks on making loans to Latinos, and then making follow-up visits to these banks to inquire about the application process itself. This activity would be implemented in English and/or Spanish, as appropriate. In a GED class, the students might feel more comfortable using only Spanish. In an ESL class, the instructor might want the students to conduct certain parts of the unit in English and provide bilingual options for other parts.

The principles and practices listed above are not meant to be exhaustive. They do provide, however, a glimpse into some of the fundamental characteristics of successful adult education practices. The implementation of these practices demands high levels of expertise on the part of the instructors. This, in turn, requires that practitioners not only have the appropriate educational qualifications upon entering a program, but that they also be provided with professional development on a continuous basis. The issue of language is particularly significant in bilingual instructional practices for Latinos. Chapter 3 presented some illustrations of bilingual workforce education programs that are currently being implemented. Some insights from the research literature that can inform educators about how two languages can be used in an instructional context were also discussed in chapter 3 under "Language Use in Bilingual Instruction." Examples of how both Spanish and English can be used in learning activities were provided in the preceding discussion of each of the principles of adult instruction. However, there is another area that must be carefully considered in the implementation of successful programs—curriculum development.

CURRICULUM DEVELOPMENT

Experienced instructors generally adapt existing textbook curricula to meet the needs and interests of their particular group of students. This is a necessity, as every group of students is unique, and regardless of how wonderful a curriculum may be, one size does not fit all. Therefore, adaptations are necessary. At times the activities or the sequence of activities will be changed, additional vocabulary may be presented, additional material will be integrated into a lesson, or a lesson will be followed up with an application of what was learned outside of the classroom. There are other times when a curriculum is provided that is incongruent with the instructor's philosophy about how students learn. Thus, it will require revisions in the approach that is presented for language learning.

But how does one go about developing a curriculum for adults that is pedagogically sound? A starting point is to become familiar with the students enrolled in a program—their needs, interests, and goals. Typically, students enrolled in a workforce education component will have job advancement and/or job placement as one of their major goals. English or biliteracy development, attainment of a GED, and an occupational credential would be subgoals relevant to the different program components they might be enrolled in. In English language-development classes, for example, a book may be purchased for the program that has a structurally based curriculum, that is, one that is centered around grammatical features of the language and that presents language in bits and pieces. An instructor in a workforce education program would know that the majority of students enrolled in the ESL class need and want to be able to use English in work-related contexts such as reading instruction manuals, filling out forms, and challenging what are considered to be unfair workplace policies. The instructor might then develop a more current, holistic curriculum that is congruent with his or her beliefs about how a second language is learned. The existing textbook might perhaps be brought in only periodically, as appropriate. Knowledge about the language demands of workers in the current economy would also be essential for the instructor to be able to develop or adapt the existing curriculum. For instructors in other components of a program, familiarity with the content framework for state or national credentials, including the GED and occupational licenses, is a must.

These curricula, although externally imposed, can also be adapted in order to fill gaps in knowledge, or to present the content in a manner that is more interesting and relevant to students. Projects such as Equipped for the Future and the National Skills Standards Board (see chapter 5) would be very useful for the purposes of content familiarity for different credentials. Frameworks for curriculum development that can be applied as one goes across diverse teaching contexts have also been identified in the research literature.

Current research in the fields of curriculum and instruction call for inquiry-based, thematic curricula, for example. Each teaching unit begins by posing a question or problem that helps to extend student understanding of a topic. This question often emerges from previous learning and is formulated collaboratively by the students and the instructor. Additional subquestions may emerge from the principal question. A series of learning activities is then designed that will help the students arrive at new understandings, which will help them answer the questions or solve the problem posed at the beginning of the unit. Such a unit will be thematic in nature; a basic theme and subthemes are explored through the learning activities that are implemented in the class.

The notion of posing a question or problem for students to solve stems from current constructivist theory about how people learn. Previous notions about learning assumed that the instructor was familiar with a body of knowledge needed to be taught to students. Learning was unidirectional, as knowledge was transferred from the instructor to the students. Materials and strategies, additionally, were often limited to textbooks, lectures, memorization of facts, and paper-pencil tests to measure how much a student had learned. Constructivist notions of learning are student-centered—they focus on student construction of new understandings that integrate prior knowledge and experiences. Learning is a multidirectional endeavor between students and the instructor, and a variety of strategies are implemented both inside and outside of the classroom. Brown (1998) writes that

Constructivism is a theory about how people learn. Based on the work of developmental psychologists, constructivism contends that people construct meaning through their interpretive interactions with and experiences in their social environments. It presumes that prior knowledge and experiences play a significant role in learning and form the basis for subsequent actions. It focuses the learner's attention on the "why" of learning and opens the door to critical thinking and intellectual development. (p. 7)

Freeman and Freeman (1998) present a set of seven questions that can be used as a guide to the development of a content-based, constructivist ESL curriculum. This simple guide is generic enough that it can also be applied to components other than ESL in workforce education programs. The guiding questions are as follows:

- What is the big question and what are the engaging smaller questions that fit into the overall theme?
- How does the question fit into the overall curricular plan, and how do the small questions support the concepts that you are trying to teach?
- How will you find out what the students already know about the question?
- What strategies will you use to explore the questions?
- What materials will you use together to explore the question?
- What steps will you and your students take to explore the question—that is, what process or learning activities will be followed?
- How will you assess student learning?

A unit that is developed according to this guide might be outlined for the VESL or ESL component of a program, as in the following sample (adapted from Colette et al., 1996). This unit would take several hours to implement. The time could be spread out over a week or more, depending on the size of the group and on the daily contact time.

Big question: What are my connections to the world of work?

Smaller questions: What is the world of work about in my family? What is the world of work about in other families? What can I learn from these work histories? How are jobs today different from those in past years? What types of jobs are available in my community? How can I get more specific information about available jobs?

Finding out what students already know: Students will brainstorm as a single group and present whatever ideas come to mind about their work experiences. The class will next fill out a KWLH chart.

Strategies: Dialoguing on the world of work, interviewing, reading, role-playing, student presentations.

Materials: Newsprint, chalkboard, reading selection, newspaper ads, government reports, assessment instruments

Learning Activities: 1. Unit will begin with a brainstorm—students will have an opportunity to share any experiences and/or knowledge related to work. The class will next fill out a KWLH chart as a group, using the big question as a guide.

2. In small groups of 4 or 5 people, students fill out an intergenerational work grid with 6 squares on newsprint that relates what type of work their grandparents did, their own and their spouse's work, and work that their sons and daughters are or may be doing in the future. The group discussions are followed by sharing time. Each group posts their grid and a member from each group reports to the class.

3. Each student interviews two family members about their positive and negative work experiences, challenges they faced, etc. Volunteers share their interview results with the class orally on the following day.

4. Each student writes a brief narrative on their family's work experiences over two or more generations.

5. Students read a short story with a topic related to an individual's work

experiences such as a selection from *16 Extraordinary Hispanic Americans* (Lobb, 1997).

6. The instructor facilitates a discussion on the story by using the Heart of Reading methodology; sample responses are modeled on the chalkboard; selected vocabulary is reviewed.

7. The class brainstorms and lists jobs that people they know perform in their community.

8. The class divides into groups and each group selects two jobs their group would like to know more about.

9. The instructor brings in excerpts or selected tables from city or county reports (for instance, employment agency or Chamber of Commerce reports) with job data from the community and distributes a report to each group. She lists four or five pieces of information that can be found in table or narrative form in each report (such as number and percent of women in the labor force, or projected growth for given occupations). She asks each group to find the information and report on it as well as on other information of interest they find in the reports.

10. Each group writes their findings on newsprint and shares with the class.

11. The class discusses the data by sharing what is of most interest to them, how the data has informed their knowledge about work, what was most surprising, etc. Each student writes a response to the data.

12. Students cut out pictures in magazines or newspapers showing people at work and also survey and cut out job postings from the newspaper.

13. Students share the pictures with the class and describe what the individual is doing.

14. The class is divided into groups. Group members share the job postings they brought and discuss what

the job might entail, qualifications, pay, etc.

15. Groups shares their information with the class.

16. The instructor presents a sample dialogue wherein a job seeker calls a business and inquires about a job posting; the content and selected grammatical structures in the dialogue are reviewed.

17. The group brainstorms and writes on newsprint additional questions and comments that might be made during a job inquiry.

18. Students are divided into pairs and asked to write a dialogue in which one student role-plays a job seeker who is calling a business about a job posting and the other role-plays a clerk who can provide general information about the job.

19. Students role play their dialogues.

20. Students are asked to select a job posting and call to ask for information on the job, or to interview a friend for information on their job.

21. Students report back to the class on the results of their inquiries.

22. Students reflect in groups on the application to them as individuals of findings from all their previous learning activities. Discussion questions are collaboratively posed (such as, "What are three steps I can take to help me get the job that I want?" or "Why is it that there are so few women as electricians and what additional challenges will I face as a Latina woman?").

Observation of student learning: Instructor assesses the student narratives that were written on their family's work histories, the student responses that were written on the city or county data about work, and the role plays that were performed in groups of two. The assessment tools that are designed include rubrics and descriptors (see chapter 5).

The curriculum outlined above integrates, as appropriate, some of the principles and practices of adult learning discussed earlier, since it is:

- Thematic (focuses on the world of work)
- Inquiry-based (poses open-ended questions)
- Constructivist (students arrive at their own understandings through reading, discussion, interviewing, etc.)
- Participatory (students participate and pose questions through dialogue, interviews, written responses)
- Integrates metacognitive skill development (students learn to summarize group ideas)
- Integrates multilevel teaching (student written work, role-plays, oral presentations are flexible as to length, complexity of content; group work is supportive of students with diverse abilities)
- Integrates technology (students may word-process written work and/or use internet for city/county job data),
- Develops critical thinking skills through the reflections and posing of questions
- Integrates assessments of student learning

This framework for curriculum development is flexible and can be adapted to the language, academic, or occupational component of a workforce education program. Despite its simplicity, however, it requires much careful planning, organization, and conceptual thinking on the part of the instructor. The assessment of student learning is one of the areas that requires particularly careful and advance planning. Assessment is integral to program accountability—and both assessment and accountability demand attention from educators, administrators, and policymakers.

5

ACCOUNTABILITY AND ASSESSMENT IN WORKFORCE EDUCATION

Accountability is an issue that has received major attention with the passage of recent legislation on adult education. The Adult Education Act that was passed in 1966 and that until recently provided guidelines in adult education gave little attention to accountability. It stated generally that programs that were funded would help adults to "acquire the basic educational skills necessary for literate functioning" (cited in Merrifield, 1998, p. 1). The lack of accountability and standards-based assessment in adult education is what some feel has been a major reason for inadequate federal funding to support these programs. Without such measures, it is difficult to determine program outcomes and nearly impossible to compare outcomes across programs, yet this information is crucial when soliciting additional funding. The lack of a cohesive accountability system also precludes the establishment of guidelines for programs that are soliciting funding. This is not to say that adult education programs have not demonstrated success, for success is evident in programs across the country that serve Latinos and other diverse groups. However, this success has for the most part been documented through an array of qualitative and quantitative measures that are deemed most appropriate by administrators in a given program, but are not standards-based.

One of the problems involved in developing a national system of accountability has been the lack of agreement on the purpose(s) of adult education and on what constitutes literacy, since literacy is integral to all forms of adult education—including workforce education. The developing notions of multiliteracies (see chapter 4) have made reaching such an agreement more complex, as has the notion of bilingual instruction for Latino adults and the interplay between the development and use of two languages in the classroom.

The passage of the Workforce Investment Act in 1998 placed accountability at the center of workforce education and has forced all involved to take a close look at their programs and how they will document successful outcomes. The act calls for four core indicators of performance, which are to be applied to states as well as to local areas. The core indicators for adults include job placement, job retention, earnings in unsubsidized employment, and skill attainment. The Secretary of Labor is to negotiate the expected levels of performance for each indicator with each state, and each state in turn is to negotiate the expected levels of performance with each local area (Jobs for the Future, 1999).

Adult education programs, however, should also be accountable to others who have a stake in these programs, including learners, instructors, program administrators, and employers. Learners have a right to know if they are participating in a quality program that meets their needs. Instructors need to know if their instructional efforts are being supported by other program components in providing needed services to students, and program administrators need to know if the curricula and program policies are effective. Employers also need to know about the quality of a program as they consider collaborative ventures with that program. There are some efforts that have been initiated at the national level in response to the need to develop program accountability. Some of these are the Equipped for the Future (EFE) project, the Adult Teaching English to Speakers of Other Languages (TESOL) Standards, the National Skills Standards Board (NSSB), and the National Reporting System (NRS).

Equipped for the Future

Equipped for the Future is a project of the National Institute for Literacy. EFF has developed standards that describe what adults need to be able to do in order to carry out their roles and responsibilities as parents and family members, citizens and community members, and workers. Stakeholders from across the country were called on to assist with this project, which began by looking at the demands and complexities of current life and how these demands have changed from previous decades. The results of the project to date are an agreement on the purposes of literacy and a set of sixteen standards that are essential for adult literacy and lifelong learning. The Secretary's Commission on Achieving Necessary Skills (SCANS) was the single previous federal effort to identify adult competencies across programs that prepared students to enter the workforce (see chapter 2). The EFF framework differs from the SCANS competencies in two ways: (1) it focuses not only on adults as workers but also as parents and citizens, and (2) rather than listing work requirements, it focuses on skills needed for effectiveness in the workplace—including the ability to cope with constant change.

EFF identifies adult literacy as meeting four purposes:

- Access to information so that adults can orient themselves in the world
- Voice to be able to express ideas and opinions
- Independent action to be able to solve problems and make decisions without relying on others
- Bridge to the future so that adults can learn how to learn and keep up with changes

The standards are organized into four skill categories: communication, decision-making, interpersonal, and lifelong learning. Additionally, key activities are listed for each standard:

Communication Skills
- Read with understanding.
- Convey ideas in writing.
- Speak so others can understand.
- Listen actively.
- Observe critically.

Decision-Making Skills
- Use math to solve problems and communicate.
- Solve problems and make decisions.
- Plan.

Interpersonal Skills
- Cooperate with others.
- Advocate and influence.
- Resolve conflict and negotiate.
- Guide others.

Lifelong Learning Abilities
- Take responsibility for learning.
- Reflect and evaluate.
- Learn through research.
- Use information and communications technology (Stein, 2000).

EFF provides workforce education programs with a set of standards that is accessible to all and that addresses the needs of a broad spectrum of students. Educators, workers, and policy-makers can identify the knowledge and skills workers need to stay current, be competitive, and move from entry level to higher-paying jobs. The framework is also said to be employer-friendly because it identifies competencies in a way that makes sense to them. EFF standards support the WIA accountability requirements, since they focus on the skills needed to enhance job retention and advancement. The next phase of the project will develop performance-based credentials that will also satisfy the accountability requirements as defined by the act.

In addition to identifying the standards for lifelong learning, the EFF designed a content framework that further elaborates on the activities that are called for across each of the three roles that adults carry out. A common activity, for example, is "to exercise rights and responsibilities." This activity is described generally and then broken down into more specific activities according to the family, citizen, and worker roles, as illustrated by the following:

Exercise rights and responsibilities: Act and advocate on behalf of yourself and others, taking into account laws, social standards, and cultural traditions.

• Recognize and assume your share of responsibilities.
• Keep updated on federal, state, and local laws.
• Make sure your behavior is just and responsible.
• Take personal responsibility to bring about change or resolve problems for the common good.

   Family Role

   • Promote values, ethics, cultural heritage within the family.
   • Support children's formal education.
   • Create a vision for the family and work to achieve it.

   Citizen Role

   • Respect others and work to eliminate discrimination and prejudice.
   • Recognize and understand human, legal, and civic rights and responsibilities.
   • Identify how to have an impact and recognize that individuals can make a difference.

   Worker Role

   • Value people different than yourself.
   • Balance individual role and needs with those of the organization.
   • Plan, renew, and pursue personal and career goals (excerpted from Stein, 2000).

This complex but comprehensive standards framework will greatly facilitate the gathering of data that can be universally accessed and used not only for accountability purposes but also for the design of curriculum that supports the standards. EFF, however, does not address the biliteracy development process of Latinos, who are often developing literacy skills in their native language as well as in English. The issue remains as to how the standards and activities can be addressed using two languages that often complement each other with respect to the social and linguistic functions in the repertoire of the speaker, and with respect to the relative proficiencies of each language. A bilingual, for example, may recognize and understand human, legal, and civic rights and responsibilities but be able to demonstrate the abilities only in Spanish. The same individual, however, may be able to use Spanish and/or English in helping a young child with school work. Thus, an enhancement of the EFF might address how the standards and content framework might be implemented with Latinos and other groups that have varying degrees of proficiency in English and the native language.

Adult TESOL Standards

Standards for programs for adults who are learning English have been recently developed by TESOL, the foremost professional organization in the field. The task force that was charged with the development of the standards consisted of instructors and program coordinators who represented a diversity of programs in the United States. The standards include a set of eight quality indicators for programs that teach English to speakers of other languages. Each indicator is described through a series of characteristics. Sample measures and performance standards are also included in order to help programs meet the accountability requirements set by WIA. The quality indicators and some of the descriptors for each are listed in the following:

- Program Structure, Administration, and Planning—The program has a curriculum, an accountability plan, and an assessment system; it provides trained personnel, demonstrates respect for the cultures of learners, and has an ongoing planning process and a technology plan.

- Curriculum—The curriculum specifies learning objectives and measurable performance outcomes and has an ongoing process for curriculum revision.

- Instruction—The instructional activities adhere to the principles of adult learning, and the approaches used meet the needs of learners with diverse backgrounds.

- Recruitment, Intake, and Orientation—The program has effective procedures for identifying and recruiting learners, has an intake process with appropriate assessment of learners' needs, goals, and language proficiencies, and has a procedure for accommodating learners waiting to enter the program.

- Retention and Transition—The program supports retention through procedures that reflect program goals, funding requirements, and learner demands; it improves retention by providing learners with appropriate support.

- Assessment and Learner Gains—The program has a comprehensive assessment policy; it uses a variety of appropriate assessments to identify learners' needs and goals in their different roles.

- Staffing, Professional Development, and Staff Evaluation—The program recruits and hires qualified staff; it has a professional development plan; it has a process for the regular evaluation of the staff.

- Support Services—The program provides access to a variety of services directly or through referrals; it provides a process for identifying learning disabilities in learners (TESOL Task Force, 2000).

These standards apply to all programs in the United States that serve adults whose first language is not English and who strive to develop communication skills in that language. This population is different from that of ABE programs. ABE enrollees do not have to struggle with the development of another language but are only developing literacy skills in their native language, English. TESOL program learners, moreover, include students with varying degrees of literacy in their native language—a factor that increases the complexity of designing a curriculum and setting time limits for meeting standards. This is a very significant issue that has an impact on Latinos with low levels of literacy in their native language, who are often unrealistically challenged to meet English literacy, academic, and occupational goals within the time periods set by TANF, NAFTA-TAA, or other workforce-education assistance programs. The TESOL standards do not recommend timelines for achievement but will provide much needed quality guidelines for literacy programs that serve Latinos who are acquiring English. Too many programs have been established in the past without the necessary administrative, curricular, or instructional planning and support that are required for this population. An increase in program quality will enhance whatever learning is accomplished within established time periods. A program self-review instrument will be developed in the future to accompany these standards.

National Skills Standards Board

The National Skills Standard's Board was created by an Act of Congress through the National Skills Act of 1994. The board comprises interest groups and volunteers from the areas of business, labor, education, civil rights, and community-based organizations that are creating and adopting a national system of skill standards for the U.S. workforce. This system will allow workers to compete effectively in today's changing economy. The skill standards will define the work to be performed within specific positions in industry, how well the work must be done, and the level of knowledge and skill required. This system "will help employers know who is qualified to fill available jobs, help employees know what skills they need to get the job they want, and help educators and trainers know how to design courses to make education and training more effective" (National Skills Standards Board, 2000, p. 2).

The skills standards will also make it easier for workers to look for employment in different states because the same set of credentials will be accepted by employers nationally. Additionally, the standards will be updated in the future as appropriate, so that they will always stay current with the demands of industry. Fifteen industry clusters have been identified that will facilitate the development of skills across a wide number of occupations. Some of these clusters are construction, education and training, health and human services, scientific and technical services, and retail trade. The federal government is playing the role of facilitator in this effort and using the necessary resources to convene the group and coordinate the work. The development of the actual standards is being done by employees, employers, and educators—those who are knowledgeable about or actually work in the field. It is expected that the inclusion of a cross-section of representatives on the board, including labor, civil rights, and community leaders, will result in fair and unbiased sets of skills that will be accessible to Latinos and other diverse groups.

National Reporting System

The National Reporting System is an outcome-based reporting system for federally funded adult education programs that are administered by the states. This project is in progress and is being conducted by the American Institutes for Research's Pelavin Research Center in Washington, D.C. The goals of the system are to establish a "national accountability system for adult education programs by identifying measures for national reporting and their definitions, establishing methods for data collection, developing software standards for reporting to the U.S. Department of Education, and developing training materials and activities on NRS requirements and procedures" (National Reporting System for Adult Education, 2000, p. 1). The NRS will improve the accountability of adult education by using a common set of outcome measures and by standardizing the data-collection system. This project originated as a result of the Government Performance and Review Act (GPRA) of 1993, which mandated that all programs develop (a) strategic plans to make sure that services were being delivered efficiently, and (b) performance indicators to demonstrate program impact.

In 1995, Congress was considering merging the adult education system into a general system of workforce development. The NRS project was the outcome of the efforts of a group of adult-education stakeholders who were advocating for the value of the adult education program separate from the workforce development system. The NRS would provide a framework that would specify the purposes of adult education programs, the characteristics of an accountability system, and seven categories of outcome measures. The project was formally designed and begun in October of 1997. The intent at that time was that participation in the NRS by adult education programs would be voluntary. That changed when WIA was passed in 1993, as this legislation established accountability requirements. The NRS is now being developed to meet the requirements of WIA. The project consists of three phases: standardization, pilot testing, and training and technical assistance. The first two phases have been completed and the project is currently in the third phase. The standardization phase developed definitions, data-collection methodologies, and software standards for data reporting. The second phase involved a small number of programs testing the definitions, collection methodologies, and the data reporting system. The third phase was begun in the summer of 1999 and will include training packets and other technical assistance to be made available to programs in order to help them implement the NRS.

The system includes three core measures that apply to all students receiving twelve or more hours of service, and a set of optional secondary measures which states are not required to report. The core measures will be accompanied by performance standards and are of three types:

- Outcome Measures—including educational gain, entered employment, retained employment, receipt of secondary diploma or GED, and placement in postsecondary education or training

- Descriptive Measures—including state demographics, reasons for attending, and student status

- Participation Measures—consisting of the contact hours received and enrollment in instructional programs for special populations or topics (such as family literacy or workplace literacy)

The educational functioning level will be used to determine educational gain under the first measure. The system has established four levels for ABE students, two for adult secondary education (ASE) students, and six levels for ESL students. Each level describes a set of competencies in literacy and numeracy. Programs assess and place students at the appropriate level upon entry, and conduct follow-up assessments in order to determine progress across the same set of levels. States can select a standardized assessment procedure to use for this purpose—a test or performance-based assessment. Additionally, the follow-up measures (such as employment or attainment of a GED) apply only to those students who designated those outcomes as goals when they entered the program (learner goals is one of the new NRS measures). For students in workforce education programs, however, job placement, retention, and the GED are goals that are expressed by virtually all of the participants.

The secondary measures include such topics as learner achievement in a work-based project, achievement of citizenship skills, and involvement in community activities and children's education. These are the types of measures that many programs have emphasized previously as evidence of success. However, this "secondary" type of data will not be considered for the awarding of grants for adult education; grants will be awarded on the basis of the core performance measures (National Reporting System for Adult Education, 2000).

The NRS places a high value on tracking people in order to report outcomes such as unsubsidized employment, career advancement, and retention. The concern has been expressed by some practitioners that this is a highly expensive endeavor. Yet, substantial funding is dependent on this data. Thus, it is difficult to get one without the other—they are both interdependent. One program reported the results of trying through telephone polling to track 200 learners who had dropped the program. They were only successful in reaching, on average, 23 percent of the people they called (Garner, 1999). Thus, in order to comply with reporting requirements under NRS, strategies that are effective and financially feasible will need to be developed for tracking people.

ASSESSMENT TOOLS

Assessment has been described as "the practices of and procedures for measuring student performance in an educational activity" (Shaw and Dowsett, cited in McKay, 1993, p. 115). The determination of the educational functioning levels of a student, as called for in the NRS, is part of an assessment procedure. Ongoing assessment of student learning is characteristic of successful classrooms. Assessment of student progress is particularly significant with Latino populations who have been away from school for decades, and who have low levels of self-confidence and high levels of anxiety upon returning to the classroom. It is important that students be able to systematically monitor their own learning and see that they are making progress, and if they are not, to be able to reflect on whatever obstacles they may be encountering in their learning and obtain assistance as needed. Instructors, too, need to reflect on the classroom practices that they are implementing and needed modifications vis-à-vis student learning. Administrators need to know if their programs are meeting the established goals and objectives. Assessment is integral to program accountability, for the assessment procedures provide a substantial part of the data for accountability purposes. There is an array of assessment tools that can be used with students, including standardized tests, nonstandardized tests (including teacher-designed tests) and performance-based assessments, which can also be standardized or nonstandardized. Four of the more widely used standardized instruments are the Comprehensive Adult Student Assessment System (CASAS), Work Keys, the Test of Adult Basic Education (TABE), the Basic English Skills Test (BEST), and the Woodcock Language Proficiency Battery (WLPB).

Comprehensive Adult Student Assessment System

The Comprehensive Adult Student Assessment System is perhaps the most widely used standardized assessment instrument in workforce education programs. CASAS is an assessment system that is validated by the U.S. Department of Education in the area of adult literacy. The system consists of three components: the curriculum competencies, the materials guide that supports instruction, and the test component. The CASAS tests may be used to place students at the appropriate level, diagnose learning needs, monitor progress, and certify student proficiency levels. The assessment instruments measure a wide range of skill levels (from pre-literacy to advanced adult secondary), and each level includes competency descriptors that elaborate on what an individual can do within that level. The system has the capacity to meet the legislative accountability requirements as defined by WIA, the NRS, the EFF, the SCANS, and other national and state initiatives.

The Workforce Learning System comprises a series of tests that was designed by CASAS specifically for workforce preparation for both native and non-native English speakers. These tests focus on employability skills—that is, the contexts of the test items are oriented to skills that an employee would need in diverse workplace settings. This system includes four key components:

- Workplace Analysis—identifies the basic skills and levels required by employers
- Workplace Appraisals—determine actual skill levels of students and provide information for establishing training
- Instructional Materials Guide—correlates over 1000 commercially available teaching resources with over 300 competency statements
- Standardized Assessments—identify learner progress, certify skill attainment, evaluate program results, and provide a reporting system (CASAS, 2001)

The standardized assessments include performance-based assessments, where students demonstrate their abilities, or competencies, through "doing" something, such as writing in a specific genre. The CASAS materials indicate that these assessments can be used to appraise a student's speaking, listening, reading, writing, and critical-thinking skills within functional contexts. The critical-thinking-skills performance appraisal is available for three areas: social studies, science, and employability. Items for employability use hypothetical situations encountered at the workplace and ask students to respond to them. An item, for example, might provide background information on toxic chemical use and then describe a situation where a chemical spill has occurred at the workplace. The student would be asked who to notify in this situation, and why. The response would be evaluated according to a rubric with benchmarks ranging from a 1 (lowest) to a 4 (highest). A 1 response would simply indicate that the foreman should be notified. A 4 response would include additional information such as the need to clear the floor, the recognition that chemical spills can be dangerous, and that only trained people should clean them (CASAS, 2001). Checklists, on which student performance is observed and recorded, are a second type of performance-based assessment. The Employability Competency System is another part of the Workforce Learning Systems. It places a heavy emphasis on rating those learner skills needed to access the labor market, such as career awareness and the ability to fill out job applications. CASAS is used extensively under TANF, WtW, NAFTA-TAA, and other workforce education programs that receive federal funding.

Work Keys

Work Keys was developed by American College Testing (ACT) to identify skill levels required by different occupations, select qualified applicants for these occupations, and communicate skill requirements to workforce instructors and future employees. The Work Keys system includes occupational profiles from diverse companies that help students and instructors to develop the required skills and skill levels. There are four components of Work Keys:

- Assessments—measure learners' workplace skills
- Job Profiling—determines the skills required for competent performance in specific jobs
- Instructional Support—helps instructors teach necessary skills
- Research and Reporting—a system that provides useful information to students.

Work Keys makes use of a common skill scale that provides the links between job profiling, assessments, and instructional support. The lowest skill level is identified as the minimum level that an employer would want in order to be interested in testing an individual for hiring purposes, and the highest level is the most complex level at which a worker would be expected to function without specialized training (CASAS, 1997).

The CASAS Workforce Learning Systems and Work Keys have been correlated so that, together, they can provide a single comprehensive system of assessment. This integrated system has been described as an "extension ladder," where CASAS provides the bottom rungs of the ladder and Work Keys provides the higher rungs. The middle of the ladder provides an overlap of rungs, where individuals in the middle of a skills-assessment continuum can be served by either or both CASAS and Work Keys. This overlap was created with the intention of providing a solid transition from the basic skills (tested by CASAS) to the more advanced skills (tested by Work Keys) as well as a solid link between the two systems (CASAS, 1997). Many workforce education programs have found the compatibility of the two systems to be very useful for measuring a wide range of skills among learners.

Test of Adult Basic Education

The Test of Adult Basic Education is published by CTB/McGraw-Hill and is a standardized assessment instrument that is widely used to assess basic skills. The test consists of a battery of multiple-choice tests and includes reading, vocabulary, writing, and mathematics sections. Programs can select which sections are given and the frequency with which students are tested on the TABE. Some programs use it to assess students regularly and others use it only initially for placement and at the end of a program to measure gains. The TABE places students into three basic levels (easy, medium, difficult), which include an upward extension for the more advanced students and a lower extension for those students with low literacy levels. The TABE is not suitable, however, for those Latinos at the very low levels of English-language proficiency, as the design of the TABE does not allow for demonstration of progress at the lower end of language development. It is appropriate for those ESL students who are at the advanced level of English-language proficiency. The test is available in Spanish, thus making it very useful for those programs with high enrollments of Latinos. The Spanish version of the TABE is frequently used to assess the skills of Latino students preparing or wanting to prepare for the GED in Spanish. The TABE Work-Related Foundation Skills (TABE-WF) and the TABE Work-Related Problem Solving (TABE-PS) are additional tests, available in English, that assess students in occupational contexts. The TABE-WF assesses the basic skills that an individual needs to be effective in a wide variety of work contexts, and the TABE-PS focuses on problem-solving tasks. The latter test is more appropriate for a student at the postsecondary level (CTB/McGraw-Hill, 2001).

Basic English Skills Test

The Basic English Skills Test, which was developed in the 1980s, is also widely used as a standardized assessment instrument for adults who are learning English. This test was developed largely as a result of the need of the Office of Refugee Resettlement for a competency-based instrument that could be consistently used across different types of resettlement programs.

The Center for Applied Linguistics in Washington, D.C. publishes the BEST and offers different forms of the test. The BEST consists of an oral interview and a literacy section. The test scores, additionally, are correlated to student performance levels that are based on existing levels developed by the programs participating in the Mainstream English Language Training Project—the project that gave rise to the BEST. The test assesses language proficiency from eight topic areas through speaking, listening, reading, and writing skills (BEST, 1984). This instrument is particularly appropriate for measuring low levels of English proficiency, as many of the test items focus on survival language such as asking for directions or telling time.

As with other standardized instruments, the BEST has its limitations in that the tests "are not sensitive enough to measure progress over short periods of time or don't contain enough items to permit learners to demonstrate fully their functional control of the language" (CAL Reporter, 2000). Van Duzer and Berdan (2000) add that the inclusion of very few items on the test that are related to each performance level along with the time constraint resulting from having to administer each test individually causes the BEST to lose its stability. This also makes the test more useful for discriminating proficiencies at the lower levels than at the higher levels. The Center for Applied Linguistics in Washington, D.C. is currently developing an updated BEST and also exploring the feasibility of a computer-assisted prototype for assessing oral proficiency.

Woodcock Language Proficiency Battery

The Woodcock Language Proficiency Battery—Revised (WLPB-R) consists of a set of individually administered tests available in English and Spanish. The tests, which provide norms for children as well as adults in both versions, measure abilities and achievement in oral language, reading, and written language. They also provide an overall measure of English or Spanish language competence. The test publishers indicate that one of the distinguishing features of the battery is its capability of determining relative strengths and weaknesses in either language through the Intra-English or Intra-Spanish discrepancies feature. This interpretation feature is based on scores from several of the individual tests, such as the oral vocabulary, letter-word identification, and dictation tests. Another feature that is said to distinguish this test is a comparative language index that allows direct comparison of Spanish and English proficiencies in a single index. The parallel tests and interpretation clusters in both the English and Spanish versions of the tests makes this possible. The WLPB-R, moreover, is designed to assess a student's proficiency in what has been called Cognitive Academic Language Proficiency (Cummins, 1989), or the form of language that is typically used in classroom learning—one that is cognitively demanding and context-reduced. This battery of tests is a revised version of the earlier WLPB that was published in 1984 (Woodcock, 1991; Woodcock and Muñoz-Sandoval, 1995).

Although traditional, standardized tests are easier and less time-consuming to administer than other forms of assessment, they have a number of pitfalls, which have been discussed in the research literature (Auerbach, 1990; García and Pearson, 1994; McKay, 1993). These instruments are intimidating to students, particularly those who have not been in a classroom for years and/or who had negative schooling experiences in their past. The mere mention of a test is often enough to cause the student to drop a program or to stay home during the testing. These traditional tests have also been found to be inherently biased because they are normed on mainstream populations—thus the test items reflect tasks, topics, and vocabulary from that same middle-class, Anglo, mainstream population. Another criticism of these tests is that they fail to capture the richness of what students know and can do and, in fact, are more reflective of test-taking skills than of actual student abilities. Because they are limited to paper and pencil, these tests also focus on literacy as a discrete set of skills rather than as a rich set of multiliteracies or practices that are rooted in social contexts (see chapter 4). They do not, for example, capture the richness of a group of displaced textile workers who have organized to open up a day-care center, nor a group of unemployed workers writing their stories about a lack of equitable assistance from government agencies and personally testifying about this before a state workforce development board. The scores that these tests yield, moreover, are just that—a set of scores. They do not provide sufficient information on student strengths or weaknesses to inform instruction and program administration.

Despite these concerns, the NRS requires that standardized instruments be utilized to assess learning gains in adult education programs that receive federal funding. However, it also provides the option of using performance-based assessments that are standardized.

PERFORMANCE-BASED ASSESSMENTS

Performance-based assessments resulted from a reform movement in public education that offered an alternative to traditional, formal tests. This reform movement originated as part of the overall systemic reform in public education over the past two decades. Alternative forms of assessment were seen as the key to liberating a curriculum that many educators felt had become very narrow and closed as a result of the standardized, multiple-choice tests that were driving it. Educators saw alternative assessment as a key to promoting a broader, more challenging curriculum that was based on current theoretical views about language, learning, and cognition, and on more authentic educational values. The move was also viewed as one that would reduce the negative effects of tests on culturally, linguistically, and economically diverse students. From this reform movement sprang alternative forms of assessment, along with an array of terms that labeled different formats of these newer assessments (García and Pearson, 1994).

Alternative assessments have been described as "any method of finding out what a learner knows or can do, that is intended to show growth and inform instruction, and is not a standardized or traditional test" (Valdez-Pierce and O'Malley, cited in Van Duzer and Berdan, 2000, p. 220). Some of the terms associated with alternative forms of assessment are "authentic," "situated," "dynamic," "portfolio," and "performance-based" assessments. Performance-based assessments are based on the traditions of art, music, and athletics, where individuals are evaluated by how well they can perform. García and Pearson (1994) write that performance-based assessments have several distinguishing characteristics:

- They represent or closely simulate performance in real-world settings.
- They are inherently entangled with instruction.
- They are grounded in the essence of the discipline.
- Scoring goes beyond a quantitative summary of a student's competence and encompasses mastery of a process (pp. 365–366).

Thus, performance-based assessments look at those tasks students can complete that are in real life or that simulate real-life activities. They are also integral to instruction—that is, the same types of learning activities that are implemented on a day-to-day basis can also serve as performance-based assessments. Written work samples, classroom presentations, and projects, for example, can be used as performance based assessments.

Performance-based assessments, however, can also be externally imposed. Externally imposed performance-based tests, for instance, have been implemented in public-school education in the states of Kentucky and Vermont. These assessments reflect the core content and processes of the different areas. For example, a performance-based assessment in science would expect that the learner would be able to "do" as a scientist does in terms of making and recording observations, gathering data, looking for patterns, and drawing conclusions. A language-related assessment might actually have the students conduct an interview, read and interpret a short story as it applies to their own lives, or write a composition. Additionally, performance-based assessments provide more than a set of scores.

Most scoring systems consist of rubrics. A rubric is a description of what must be demonstrated at various levels of success. Points are generally assigned to each level of the rubric in order to develop a scale. Thus, a rubric for a classroom presentation may range from a 1 (indicating that the student presentation was poorly organized and lacked content) to a 6 (indicating that the student did an excellent job of delivering the presentation and that the presentation included substantive content). Checklists are also widely used in performance-based assessments. These include lists of what a student can do that are checked off as the learner demonstrates performance of a given task. Figures 5.1 and 5.2 provide examples of performance-based assessments using a rubric and a checklist, respectively. Checklists may or may not be assigned point values. The checklist in figure 5.2, for example, could have a total of 10 points, where each item counts for

Figure 5.1
Performance-Based Rubric—Memo Writing: Reporting an Accident at Work

3	Memo is well written: 1. Content includes all six pieces of essential information: employee name, date of memo, date and time of accident, description of the accident, description of the injury, and name(s) of witnesses. 2. No grammatical errors; no spelling errors 3. Appropriate memo format is used
2	Memo is comprehensible: 4. Content is missing no more than three of the essential pieces of information 5. Some grammatical and spelling errors 6. Appropriate memo format is used
1	Memo is poorly written: 7. More than three of the essential pieces of information are missing 8. Multiple errors in grammar and spelling make it incomprehensible in some areas 9. There are some errors in the format used
0	Memo was not done

Figure 5.2
Performance-Based Checklist—Patient Intake Process

☐   cross-checked patient name with date of birth on file

☐   greeted patient

☐   inquired about and recorded purpose of visit

☐   inquired about and recorded any symptoms of illness

☐   took and recorded blood pressure reading

☐   took and recorded pulse count

☐   took and recorded temperature reading

☐   took and recorded weight

☐   escorted patient to appropriate examining room

☐   placed patient file in waiting holder

1 point. Because rubrics are descriptive, they provide information in terms of learner strengths or weaknesses, which can assist the instructor in designing curriculum and the student in monitoring progress towards stated goals. Performance-based assessments have been widely used to assess classroom learning in adult education at a local level. However, they have not been used to satisfy accountability requirements by funding agencies because they do not meet the standardization requirements. Another reason for not using them is that they require a considerable investment of time as well as experience on the part of educators to implement them on a large scale.

The challenge for adult as well as public-school education has been to develop and refine performance-based assessments that are standardized and suitable for large-scale implementation. Many adult education programs utilize traditional, standardized tests that satisfy accountability requirements (such as CASAS and BEST) and complement them with performance-based assessments at the program level. The latter are then used to gather information about the learners that is more diagnostic and can inform instruction. Different standardized instruments that lead to credentialing are also integral to workforce education programs and their outcomes. However, there are often no options in this area because of national and state requirements. The academic component of a program, for instance, will administer the GED practice tests, and when the students are deemed ready they will take the official GED test. Likewise, a student in a medical-assistant program must be prepared to pass the exam at the state level. A truck driver must pass the driving test as well as a written test, also at the state level.

Regardless of the instruments that are used, accountability and assessment in workforce education programs that receive federal funding will now be largely driven by NRS guidelines that support the WIA reporting requirements. The NRS provides options in several areas related to accountability and assessment. The system does not, for example, (a) require a specific type of record system or software, (b) specify a specific assessment or test, (c) preclude using additional educational functioning levels, (d) preclude collecting other measures, nor (e) specify the skill areas in which to teach or assess students. However, in reality, it will be difficult for programs to exercise most of these options because of limited resources. Selecting an alternative system of record-keeping or software can be a costly choice, since NRS is providing technical assistance and packets only for the selected system of record-keeping and software. Although performance-based assessments are possible, they must be standardized (discussed in the following section). The collection of other measures not required by NRS is also a possibility, but highly unlikely, because of already strained adult-education budgets—not to mention that only the specified core measures will be considered for funding. Thus, at present, there are really no choices left, except the ability of programs to teach in the areas that they wish, and assess educational gains in these areas. One positive factor of the NRS system is that it has finer gradations in the education-functioning levels. The ESL category includes a new intermediate level, which was formed by breaking up the old beginning and intermediate levels. Thus, it will increase the probability of demonstrating the progress of those Latinos who come into a program with lower levels of proficiency in English.

Standardization and Quality Enhancement of Alternative Assessments

A standardized performance-based assessment basically means that the procedure must be standardized—that is, the way in which the assessment is presented and scored must be consistent. Del Vecchio, Gustke, and Wilde (1998) indicate that a standardized testing procedure is one in which (a) written and oral instruction, (b) specific items, (c) length of testing and time of testing, (d) method of scoring, and (e) the purpose for the assessment are the same each time the instrument is used. They add that "only with a standardized procedure can the results of the instrument be compared from one administration to the next, from one group of students to the next" (pp. 346–347). However, they also caution that standardization does not, in and of itself, make for a high quality instrument. It is suggested that alternative assessments ensure validity, reliability, and inter-rater criteria in order to enhance the quality of the assessments particularly when the stakes are high.

Validity and reliability are also applied to traditional forms of testing. Validity describes the degree to which an assessment measures what it claims to measure. Alternative assessments can increase validity by making sure that the results (a) provide an accurate picture of how well a student knows the targeted proficiency or achievement, (b) are based on at least five different tasks measuring similar skills, and (c) are generalizable to other tasks to ensure mastery. Reliability refers to the consistency of a score upon repeated administrations of an assessment or upon having the assessment scored by a different person. To increase reliability in an alternative assessment, it is recommended that (a) multiple tasks leading to the same outcome be designed, (b) trained judges who are working with clear scoring criteria be used, and (c) monitoring be done periodically to ensure that the criteria are being used consistently by the raters—that is, to ensure inter-rater reliability (Del Vecchio, Gustke, and Wilde, 1998).

In order to establish inter-rater reliability, there is a series of steps that must be followed:

- Agree on the criteria that will be used to assess student's work or behavior
- Select student work as sample scoring materials
- Practice scoring the samples of work using the same criteria and the same rating or scoring form
- Compare the scores to determine the extent of agreement on the scoring criteria
- Score independently, with frequent reliability checks to avoid inconsistencies in the rating process. (Del Vecchio, Gustke, and Wilde, 1998, p. 348)

The ratings are compared and clarified through the process until the raters achieve a desired level of consistency on the scores for given samples of student work (usually 80 percent or above). This straightforward process ensures accuracy in the scoring results of performance-based assessments.

In order to exercise the option of using performance-based assessments under the NRS, the assessments must, at minimum, go through the long process of establishing the consistency, or standardization, of the procedure as described above. However, in order to ensure a higher quality; in the instruments; validity, reliability, and inter-rater reliability, should also be established for the assessments. The field of adult education is not yet at the point where performance-based assessments have been developed that are standardized and can be applied on a large scale. The exception to this is in the evaluation of a single type of writing—compositions—such as those that students are asked to write for the GED test. However, this type of writing represents a single genre of writing that is not widely applicable or relevant to student lives outside of the classroom.

In discussing the use of alternative assessments in adult literacy, Wrigley (2001) writes that these assessments have not matured enough to be used as a means of reporting and aggregating learner gains. She states that these approaches have remained at a local level because "there has not been enough field testing to establish the reliability of these measures and there have not been sufficient efforts to implement alternative assessments across programs" (p. 1). Wrigley advocates for the development of an alternative assessment system that can both serve accountability purposes and improve programs. One suggestion provided is to create profiles of students that capture basic background variables (such as age and years of schooling) as well as rich descriptive information (such as current literacy practices and learner goals). These profiles, or running records, would need to be accompanied by rubrics, scales (to indicate where student abilities fall on a continuum), and benchmarks. Thus, the future use of alternative assessments to satisfy accountability requirements will first require a substantial investment of time and money for research and development. The EFF and TESOL Standards initiatives mentioned earlier are two such efforts that have already begun to develop performance-based assessments. The EFF assessment framework will be linked to the EFF standards and to the NRS. This assessment tool will integrate the four dimensions of learning as identified in the research literature on how people learn: knowledge base in the area, fluency in task completion, independence in task completion, and range (or level) of performance (National Research Council, 2000). The hope is that this work will impact the NRS system when it comes up for review in the year 2005.

Thus, the challenge for educators in this area is to further develop performance-based and other types of alternative assessments that are standardized, that can provide much more descriptive information about learners' knowledge and capabilities, and that can be implemented on a large scale across programs. This type of information will allow for cross-program documentation of success and will provide the type of information sought by funding agencies and others who also have a stake in accountability. The development of alternative assessment systems is particularly crucial for Latinos and other linguistically and culturally diverse groups whose abilities have been underrepresented by traditional forms of standardized testing. Alternative forms of assessment, most significantly, can better capture student abilities because they are not bound to paper-pencil, verbal forms of demonstrating knowledge but can also be tied to behaviors or the evaluation of products resulting from behaviors. Additionally, alternative assessments that entail more language dependency can be designed in Spanish and/or English, as appropriate, in order to allow Latinos to demonstrate a wide range of abilities and knowledge. The ability to estimate and justify estimations in certain types of problem-solving, for instance, can be probed in either language, as can the ability to make operational or human-management types of decisions by a medical assistant or a childcare worker. The performance-based assessment in Figure 5.2, for example, is based on behavior, with the exception of recording the readings and symptoms of illness in the patient file.

Another promising approach to the areas of assessment and accountability has been taken by educators who have advocated for a system that focuses not on outcomes of a program (such as student achievement), but rather on those characteristics that make for a high-quality teaching and learning experience. Such a system would look at inputs rather than outcomes in determining program quality. The focus, for example, would be on teacher preparation, curriculum, use of technology, and materials. The notion of looking at program quality is not a new one, although the idea of using it for accountability purposes is innovative. The 1992 revisions of the National Education Act created a mandate that required all states to develop and adopt Indicators of Program Quality and to use them to monitor program effectiveness. The indicators were often comprehensive in terms of the program areas that were examined. The Indicators of Program Quality for workforce literacy for the state of Texas, for example, examined five program areas:

- Learner Outcomes—includes the preparation of students in terms of academic knowledge, lifelong learning skills, and workforce development proficiencies

- Program Planning—includes the implementation of needs assessment for program planning and formative and summative evaluations

- Curriculum and Instruction—includes teaching processes that are learner-centered, participatory, dynamic, based on a work-related framework, and that integrate problem-solving skills and holistic assessment

- Professional Development—includes a plan that is collaboratively developed and consistent with holistic instruction

- Student Retention—the program retains employees and participants long enough for them to achieve their goals (Texas Workforce Commission, nd)

These indicators have been used by some programs at the local level for self-assessment.

Comings (1999) advocates using input measures based on these indicators of program quality to develop a system of accountability. He explains the rationale for this approach to accountability:

- It is a system that has already been used successfully in higher education, where professional teams visited a college or university and looked at characteristics such as faculty preparation and use of technology within a program in order to renew or award accreditation.

- States have already developed indicators of program quality, which already provide criteria for looking at inputs that could easily be turned into measures that could be documented and observed.

- Standardized measures such as the CASAS do not always reflect the curriculum that is being delivered in a classroom, nor do they capture important student outcomes.

- Measuring the impact of programs on student lives is often negatively affected by factors outside of the program's control, such as a downward spiral in the economy, making it unjust in these cases to penalize programs for low impact.

Comings (1999) adds that a research component could be added to prove that participation in these programs is leading to success: "Achievement and impact should be measured by careful studies that have the resources to assess academic skills and to look at impact over several years" (p. 8). The use of quality indicators for accountability purposes is most promising, therefore, in that there is already a foundation in place for this process that could be extended and refined.

The tasks and challenges that lie ahead in the areas of assessment and accountability are formidable, but they can and should be dealt with in order to provide a more equitable system for Latinos and other diverse groups. An equitable system of assessment would capture the richness of student achievement and learning both inside and outside of the classroom, and would include both the "core" and "secondary" measures as defined by the NRS. An equitable accountability system would also be based on the concept of mutuality. Merrifield (1999) indicates that such a system would, among other things, be

negotiated between the stakeholders in a process that engages all the players in clarifying expectations, designing indicators of success, negotiating information flows, and building capacity . . . [and] each responsibility is matched with an equal, enabling right; the right to a program that meets one's learning needs with the responsibility to take learning seriously, for example. (p. 9)

The success of NRS reporting requirements as a catalyst for the further development and refinement of performance-based and other forms of alternative assessments on a national level remains to be seen.

6

WORKFORCE EDUCATION FOR LATINOS: POLICY RECOMMENDATIONS

Workforce education for the Latino workforce has been problematic because of a number of political, economic, and educational issues. Education, however, remains the key to progress for Latinos. This chapter presents recommendations on policy for government, for industry, and for educational administrators.

RECOMMENDATIONS FOR GOVERNMENT

Work is at the center of current legislation in the areas of adult education and economic assistance. Welfare reform, for instance, emphasizes a Work First approach. In order to receive full TANF funding, states must place a certain percent of welfare participants into jobs or work activities as defined by the state, and individuals must work a prescribed number of hours each week. The percentage of clients working must also increase each year until it reaches 50 percent in 2002. The emphasis on Welfare-to-Work is on helping the most disadvantaged welfare recipients in their transition to work. The Workforce Investment Act, which replaced the Adult Education Act, reinforces the connection between adult education and work. This act, moreover, calls for the creation of workforce investment boards at the local level to create education plans. The result of these developments is that clients are pressured into taking the first job that becomes available, and they are filling positions that pay low wages and keep families in poverty. Additionally, once they begin to work, there are few if any opportunities for continuing their education and advancing to jobs that pay better wages. Work First is being emphasized despite the fact that studies have indicated that these same people who seek welfare assistance and are placed into jobs are also those who have the lowest levels of literacy. Research data, for example, has revealed that Hispanic adults reported the fewest years of schooling in the United States of all racial/ethnic groups (National Center for Education Statistics, 1996). Therefore, the first policy recommendation is that the emphasis must change from work first to one that integrates work with education. This does not preclude short-term skills training that can quickly provide a job and provide some security to families. However, provisions must be made that will encourage clients to continue their education. Education for the long term, which will provide a GED plus a postsecondary credential, must be the goal. In his research, Grubb (1996) found that the premium for completing high school has increased substantially, so that dropouts are being left further and further behind in terms of earnings. The high-school diploma or GED is the only subbaccalaureate credential required for virtually every position that he examined in the mid-skilled labor market. Thus, assistance for GED attainment is crucial for Latinos, even if they are able to find jobs that do not require it, because in the long run the GED will be the key to continued education and better jobs. The GED would be followed by the attainment of a postsecondary credential that would provide a foundation for continued education and/or professional growth, such as a state license and/or an associate's two-year degree. This might include, for example, a medical assistant license, or a child-development associate's degree.

Postemployment follow-up must be a part of the provisions and must include support services such as transportation, medical benefits, and childcare that last at least long enough for the transition to unsubsidized full-time employment. Postemployment services will enhance job retention and/or a transition to postsecondary education.

Policy must also be more inclusive of Latinos and other ethnic groups. That is, federal initiatives must stop working within an English, mainstream-centered model of workforce education and provide adequate funding for ESL and bilingual instruction for adults. The demographic realities in the United States are that Latinos make up the largest ethnic group, and many of them are not proficient enough in English to fill higher-paying jobs. Employers are calling for increased communication skills in English, and language proficiency takes time to develop. In addition to job training and education, Latinos face the additional challenge of acquiring a second language. Yet, the amounts of time that are provided in many programs, including those for displaced workers, do not allow additional time and economic assistance for workers to develop their English skills. Certain programs, such as Welfare-to-Work, do not cover ESL as stand alone instruction.

The current time limitations and entanglement of different funding streams that a student might be receiving are also problematic in that they preclude some students from completing a program through to the attainment of a postsecondary credential. For example, a group of students that participated in an informal interview with the author and an adult education administrator on workforce education instruction explained that they were provided assistance through the completion of coursework in basic-care attendance but were cut off at the point at which they had to study to pass the state examination for a license as a certified nurse's assistant because their funding sources had "run out." Yet, employment in a healthcare area, such as in a nursing home, is dependent on the license. The students could not afford to study and pay for the exam without government assistance. Thus, they were essentially dropped at a point when they were close to attaining the key to job security and further education. All parties in this case lost from this policy. The educators were not able to see their students attain the credential that they were working toward, the students did not reap the full benefits of their efforts, and government increased the probability of seeing them again on an assistance program. A step in the right direction would be to look at the design of successful family literacy programs (see Huerta-Macías, in press) when planning workforce education programs. These models have been designed with the well-being of families at their center, rather than work first. They also provide an integrated array of instructional and support services that help students overcome barriers to achievement. Services in these programs include but are not limited to ESL instruction for parents, childcare, and transportation.

Thus, a workforce education model that integrates short-term job-skills training, but that has as a goal the attainment of a credential past the GED rather than work first, is essential if Latinos are to climb the economic ladder. Such a model would integrate pre- and post-employment support services and would include the attainment of a postsecondary credential, bilingual instruction, on-the-job training, and higher education as a long-term goal. Table 6.1 provides a framework for an integrated bilingual model for workforce education for Latinos.

The model that is proposed would be a collaboration between industry, educators, and government. It integrates an occupational, a basic skills/ESL, and an academic component, each of which would utilize Spanish and/or English in the delivery of instruction. Four benchmarks are also integrated into the plan as indicators of student progress. The model would provide financial assistance for study and counseling, childcare, and transportation as support services until a student attained a postsecondary credential or license. It also has provisions for short-term job training in an occupation that provides an opportunity for growth, advancement, and employment in a demand area in the labor market. A student following this plan would be studying on a full-time basis until the

Table 6.1
Integrated Bilingual Workforce Education Program Model

Intake: assessment of student interests, needs, biliteracy skills, orientation to program & benefits, etc.

Time Sequence	Occupational Component (Spanish and English)	Basic Education & Literacy Component	Academic Component (Spanish and/or English)	Support Services
Phase I	job skills training	basic skills and/or ESL	GED study	counseling, transportation, child care
Benchmark A	apprenticeship readiness			
Phase II	part-time apprenticeship and job skills training w/prospective employer	continued ESL instruction	continued GED study as appropriate	counseling, transportation, child care
Benchmark B	completion of job skills coursework	completion of ESL coursework		
Phase III	full time employment plan with integrated study component toward post-secondary credential	on the job ESL learning	continued GED study as appropriate	counseling & partially subsidized transportation, child care (stipends)
Benchmark C			attainment of GED	
Phase IV	full time employment plan with integrated study component toward post-secondary credential	on the job ESL learning		counseling & partially subsidized transportation, child care (stipends)
Benchmark D	attainment of post-secondary credential or license			
Phase V	option for 24 months continued post-secondary study with subsidized tuition; unsubsidized full time employment			

first benchmark of apprenticeship readiness was reached. At that point, he or she would have acquired enough skills to function successfully as an apprentice, or intern, in a given occupation. Meanwhile, study would continue on a half-time basis until completion of course-work in the occupational, ESL, and academic components. A second benchmark would be reached with the completion of the occupational course-work, at which time the student would be hired on a full-time basis. At this point, childcare and transportation would not be fully subsidized, but assistance for these services would be provided in the form of stipends. Meanwhile, GED study would continue for approximately two hours per day. The employer would contribute one hour and the employee another hour (a tax credit or other incentive might be negotiated for the employer's contribution of time). Upon completion of ESL and GED course-work, English language learning would continue on the job, within the context of the particular occupation. A third benchmark would be the attainment of the GED. The fourth benchmark would be reached when the student acquired a postsecondary credential or license, preferably in a program of study that is articulated with a program for more advanced study in the same area. This might be, for example, a certified nurse's assistant license, or a child-development associate's degree. At that point subsidies for support services would cease. However, the student would be encouraged to continue postsecondary studies by being given tuition assistance for a maximum of 24 months. This would provide an opportunity for someone with a certified nurse's assistant license, for instance, to study in a program for a vocational nursing license that could at a later point in time be articulated with a two- or four-year nursing degree. Likewise, an individual with training in plastic injection molding would have the opportunity to complete a certificate in plastics technology and then an Associate of Applied Science degree in the same field. The tuition would be provided in the form of Pell grants or other types of grants that would cover vocational as well as academic programs of study. This plan would have the following benefits:

- It would provide options and facilitate the long-term goal of education via a postsecondary credential, as well as the short-term goal of job-skills training.

- Postemployment support services and counseling would increase the probability of program completion by students.

- Limitations on government program assistance would be based on attainment of benchmarks and satisfactory progress rather than on time limits only. Thus, assistance would not be cut when students who were successfully progressing in their studies were close to attaining a postsecondary credential.

- The integrated as opposed to sequential curriculum model would allow a student to progress more quickly through the program, increase motivation levels, and increase the probability of completion.

- The bilingual model would also enhance progress and probability of program completion, would be pedagogically sound from the educational perspective, and would be more equitable from the political perspective than an English-only model.

- Through the apprenticeship, employers would have the opportunity of developing the job-specific skills they need, would have the benefit of developing familiarity and rapport with the employee, and would be more likely to acquire employee loyalty and productivity.

- Students would have the benefit of learning both an occupation and developing English language skills on the job, and their motivation and self-esteem would increase as a result of their relatively quick re-entry into employment.

- Students would have some financial security through job-skills training, and increased security as they reached the various benchmarks.

- Government would benefit in the long term from lower unemployment levels since job retention would most likely increase (that is, the revolving-door problem would be lessened).

- Government program assistance for a longer term would be offset by decreased numbers on the welfare rolls as a result of better wages.

- Educators and industry would benefit from a close partnership that would be developed from the enhancement of both education and job-skills training through the contextualized learning at the work site, and job performance would be enhanced through occupational, language, and academic course-work.

- The half-time study-class schedule would be more likely to allow increased staff development time for educators, and thus more effective teaching and learning experiences in the course-work provided.

- The community and all of society would benefit from increased education and employment levels among Latinos.

- The focus on education through a strong partnership between industry, government, and educators, along with support services, would be more equitable because it would work toward closing the achievement gaps between Latinos and Whites.

An accountability system that recognizes progress at all levels of achievement and is learner- as well as knowledge-centered is also essential. The current evaluation system places an accountability emphasis on unsubsidized job placement. This, in effect, discourages states from placing clients in longer-term educational programs. Instead, it gives states an additional incentive for placing them into the first job that is available, regardless of whether it is a dead-end, low-paying job. The EFF and Adult TESOL assessment frameworks appear to be most promising and could be integrated into the workforce education model that is proposed. A strong performance-based assessment system that is valid and reliable would help determine satisfactory student progress (and thus eligibility for continued financial support) towards the attainment of a credential. The reliance on assessment of progress for continued funding, rather than on time limitations, would provide a more equitable system for Latino workforce education. The credential-based, rather than time-based, model is critical if Borderland and other Latino populations that have low levels of formal education and literacy are to be provided with an equitable opportunity to reach their educational goals.

Funding sources, moreover, must be better coordinated by the states. The One-Stop centers are a step in the right direction in their provision of an umbrella of services under one roof. However, the different programs remain fragmented and confusing to a large extent. TANF, for example, is not required to be a part of these centers. Yet, their clients are now treated as job seekers, and therefore workforce education has also become integral to TANF. Unemployed Latinos need to be able to access all of the services that they qualify for, including TANF, Welfare-to-Work, and NAFTA-TAA funds. Even though the clients that seek assistance under these programs may be somewhat different in terms of their experiences and skills, they are all looking for job skills and an education that will help them progress from their current circumstances. Knowledge about the client, communication among key staff, and familiarization with all available resources for workforce education are essential for referring workers to the appropriate programs. Thus, not only must the funding sources be located under one roof, but the delivery of services must also be integrated in order to provide economic and educational assistance that is truly seamless. Students should be able to transition from one program, or phase of development, to another smoothly and effortlessly.

Streamlining must also occur at the federal level. The many funding streams with different compliance criteria must be currently untangled by administrators at the state and local levels. The integration of services should also be helpful in streamlining the eligibility and compliance criteria in a way that makes sense to administrators and clients. The criteria and compliance guidelines across programs should be easily accessible to educational program administrators as well. At present, educators generally understand only those small pieces that they deal with and are unable to help students who face barriers as they seek the different avenues of assistance that are available. Students are left frustrated by not being able to find personnel who can actually help them navigate through the various channels of assistance. The result is that they get bounced from office to office, often with conflicting information, as they seek assistance from diverse programs. A small number of "federal assistance coordinators" who would be available at the One-Stops would be helpful. These coordinators would be knowledgeable about the various programs, their interfaces, and their eligibility criteria—and they would be available for consultation with workers.

Another essential factor for Latino access to services is personnel who are fluent in Spanish. Spanish-speaking staff must be available within every agency or program represented in the One-Stops. The research literature indicates that Spanish-speaking personnel are sometimes not available even in areas with high concentrations of Latinos.

Finally, government must work closely with industry in an effort to prevent plant closings and layoffs, and/or to provide adequate notification when the layoffs are inevitable. Currently, the emphasis is on compensation once employees are laid off (for example, through NAFTA-TAA funds), and legislation such as the Worker Adjustment and Retraining Notification (WARN) act is difficult to enforce because of loopholes. Collaboration between government and industry is essential in order to remedy this and to arrive at agreements that are beneficial to all involved.

RECOMMENDATIONS FOR INDUSTRY

As discussed above, industry must collaborate with government entities in order to negotiate outcomes that are favorable to all parties when plant closings or layoffs seem imminent. Industry must also be willing to contribute to postemployment training and education for workers so that they have the opportunity to advance within a company. The employers in the proposed model would contribute sixty minutes of time off during the work day for classes. Additional contributions could also be made, such as providing classrooms at the work site, hiring a GED instructor, purchasing materials, and/or subsidizing stipends for childcare for their full-time employees. Collaboration must also take place between industry and educators in order to negotiate apprenticeship and full-time employment upon completion of training and education. Currently, learners are generally recruited for training programs and often use their maximum allowable benefits only to find upon completion of the program that there are few openings in a given area or that, for other reasons, it is very difficult to gain entry into specific areas of business. Negotiations between industry and educators that provide a commitment to employment of the learner on the part of industry is essential, as is a commitment to certain levels of education and training on the part of educators once a learner completes a program. This type of networking between educators and industry has been the key to successful programs such as Motivation Education and Training described in chapter 3.

Industry must also be realistic about the levels of English proficiency that are required for specific jobs. Studies have found that some employers include English proficiency as a requirement for jobs that, in effect, do not require much communication with the public or other entities. Some service and healthcare-related jobs are examples of this. Including English-language proficiency as a blanket requirement is counterproductive for an employer who might otherwise be able to hire a worker with a strong work ethic as well as other desirable qualities, such as maturity, loyalty, responsibility, and oral proficiency and literacy skills in Spanish. The changing demographics of the United States, which include increasing numbers of large communities that are Latino concentrated, further attest to the social reality that residents in the United States can function successfully in their daily life using only Spanish. Additionally, employers must acknowledge that general educational attainment is not specific to language. That is, too often a lack of English language proficiency is equated with low levels of literacy and knowledge. Employees with knowledge and skill qualifications must not be bypassed because they are not fully proficient in English. The recognition and valuing of Spanish as a language of the United States is an ideological change that must take place among industry, government, and educators. Change will be slow and difficult in this area, because recognition and valuing of Spanish as a language of business and education in this country would also mirror a change in power relations between mainstream and minority groups. Still, the privileging of Spanish is something to struggle for if Latinos in the United States are to advance and receive full benefits from society for their participation as workers, family and community members.

Industry must also collaborate closely with educational program administrators in planning curriculum and instruction that will best meet the needs and interests of both learners and employers. Job-specific skills may be a part of such programs, but employers, program administrators, and learners must all buy into the ultimate goal of education that will make a difference for Latinos in terms of climbing up the economic ladder and for employers in terms of job-related qualities. It is essential to recognize, for example, that in the long run employees with higher levels of education and increased communication, technological, reasoning, and other skills will ultimately benefit the employer and all of society as well.

Research has shown that employer discrimination against Latinos continues to exist (Perez, 2000). In order to address this, industry must implement recruiting, hiring, and on-the-job practices that are equitable. Workplace injustices against Latinos, and all ethnic groups must stop, and employees must be better informed through One-Stop centers and other government entities of their legal rights in this area. Additionally, employees must be provided with legal support in cases where this is necessary, for it is of little use to inform employees of their legal rights and employers of possible sanctions if funding for enforcement is unavailable.

RECOMMENDATIONS FOR EDUCATORS AND PROGRAM ADMINISTRATORS

Strong partnerships with industry are essential for the workforce educational model that is proposed. Negotiations for the hiring of workers as apprentices and as full-time employers upon completion of required education and/or training can be highly motivational and beneficial for all involved. It is crucial, however, that educators also advocate for and support postemployment education toward the GED and a postsecondary credential that will allow workers to advance economically, personally, and professionally.

Professional development must be provided to instructors on a continuous basis so that they stay abreast of current theory and practice, including the integration of technology to enhance learning. Traditionally, instructors are provided with training at the beginning of a program and then left on their own. A single intensive series of workshops is not as useful for the practitioner as ongoing assistance throughout the teaching period. This does not imply bringing outside experts in for talks with the teaching staff. Professional development can be most successful when it is generated from within an organization or program. This can be done in diverse ways. Simply providing some time on a regular basis for the teaching staff to meet, share ideas, strategies, and materials, and discuss professional readings can be extremely helpful and motivating for all involved. These groups can be led on a turn-taking basis by different leaders or master teachers within the program who are also responsible for suggesting and distributing professional readings of interest for discussion. Equally important is that the teaching staff be paid for this time, as well as for additional preparation time. Other professionals, including those in business, are not expected to engage in professional development during their personal time; instructors should not be expected to do this either. Adequate preparation time is a must for high-quality instruction, and it is just that instructors be respected as professionals and be compensated for this time.

Administrators and instructors, collaboratively with industry and government entities, must develop assessment plans that satisfy the need for accountability on the part of all involved. Adult education programs, including those with the same or similar goals, have traditionally not had a single system or framework for accountability. Unsubsidized job placement appears to be the area of emphasis in the current accountability systems for workforce education and training, including that provided through TANF, WIA, WtW, and NAFTA-TAA. However, the vision for workers must be broader. Educators must have postsecondary education, as opposed to short-term training, as a goal. Education that provides a minimum of a GED plus a postsecondary credential or license in an occupational area that promises growth and advancement opportunities is the key to economic mobility. Conversely, short-term training by itself often provides no more than a revolving door where workers go out and back into TANF, or where they find themselves still unemployed and/or living in poverty even after exhausting their benefits. Education past the GED is crucial for Latinos, who have the highest high-school dropout rates, who are filling low-wage jobs at increasing rates, who are the most youthful of the population, and thus most likely to be participating in the workforce.

The challenges for Latinos are multiple and include not only the acquisition of a second language but general knowledge and literacy skills, given that they tend to have the lowest levels of schooling—often not surpassing four years within given segments of the population. Celebration of short-term goals or benchmarks as part of their larger goals can be highly motivational and helpful in keeping the learning on track for the attainment of specific objectives.

It is also incumbent upon educators to familiarize workers with the employability market within their communities. Workers need to know what types of jobs are available, job requirements, the types of salaries and benefits provided, and opportunities for advancement. Keeping abreast of the market requires close and continuous communication with industry. Grubb (1996) found that some employers castigate occupational programs for concentrating on specific skills to the detriment of more general or academic capacities. He stresses the need for developing the more specific entry-level skills that workers need to obtain a job, but also for developing the academic, more general competencies that they will need for promotion and mobility in the long run. Thus, collaborative planning of the curriculum between industry and educators is essential to designing a program that will best meet the needs and interests of both workers and employers.

Workers must also be taught job-search skills that are most effective. Current research (Perez, 2000) indicates that Latinos tend to rely on close networks of family and friends to find jobs. This often puts them at a disadvantage; they need to know how to sell and market themselves to prospective employers. Studies indicate that discrimination against Latino workers still exists (Perez, 2000). Thus, it is essential that educators advocate for the inclusion of workers' rights and self-advocacy in their curricula. If the purpose of education is positive transformation (including economic mobility), then workforce education curricula must include critical perspectives with respect to the workplace. Topics such as workmen's compensation, rights to occupational safety equipment, filing grievances against employers (including harassment), and language rights on the job must be integrated into curricula. Any curriculum that does not include discussion of these types of topics falls short of the ultimate goal of bringing about positive transformation in the lives of workers and their families.

Freire (1985) discusses the notion that illiterates are not in and of themselves marginal but rather are oppressed members of the dominated strata of society. He adds, "If then, marginality is not by choice, marginal man has been expelled from and kept outside of the social system and is therefore the object of violence" (p. 48). Latinos as well as other minority groups have been marginalized by public-school and adult-education systems that have provided instruction in a language that is often not understood. Additionally, these systems have imposed a structure on Latinos that ignores the social reality of educational inequities, which have precluded many from obtaining a basic education and from developing basic literacy skills. In Freire's words, Latinos have been the object of violence by mainstream policies and practices. Yet, the unemployed and/or displaced workers who now seek to advance themselves have contributed greatly to the prosperity of this country through their labor in manufacturing and other industries that, perhaps, are now dwindling in the face of new technologies. They continue to provide us, moreover, with services in such industries as food and healthcare that are often an indispensable part of our lives. It is time, then, that Latino adults be provided with equitable opportunities through access to educational programs that meet their needs and interests. There is no better time, furthermore, than the current one, as adult education is receiving more attention than in years past and as Latinos continue to make their presence more strongly known in all areas from art to politics. As Verdecia (2001) states, "Hispanics are here to stay. The sensible reaction is to approach this reality with more wisdom than fear. Corporate America, for instance, needs to reach out to our people—for real. Not under the flag of political correctness. Not under the hypocritical, often meaningless slogan of diversity" (p. 8). The same can be said for government, industry, and educators; all need to reach out to Latinos—for real. Education must be first.

References

American Educational Research Association. (1992). *Educational researcher: Special issue on bilingual education.* Washington, D.C.: Author.

Auerbach, E.R. (1990). *Making meaning, making change.* Boston, MA: University of Massachusetts English Family Literacy Project.

Auerbach, E.R. (1993). Reexamining English only in the ESL classroom. *TESOL Quarterly* 27(1), 9–52.

Auerbach, E.R. (1996). *Adult ESL/literacy: From the community to the community: A guidebook for participatory literacy training.* Mahwah, NJ: Lawrence Erlbaum Associates.

Auerbach, E.R. (1999). From the chair. *Adult education newsletter* [official publication of the adult education interest section, Teachers of English to Speakers of other Languages]. Alexandria, VA: TESOL.

Auerbach, E.R. and N. Wallerstein. (1987). *ESL for action: Problem-posing at work.* Reading, MA: Addison-Wesley Longman.

Baba, M.L. (1991). The skill requirements of work activity: An ethnographic perspective. *Anthropology of Work Review* 12(3), 2–11.

Baker, C. (1996). *Foundations of bilingual education and bilingualism.* Avon, England: Multilingual Matters Ltd.

Barker, G.C. (1972). *Social functions of language in a Mexican-American community.* Tucson, AZ: University of Arizona Press.

Barton, P.E. (1999). *What jobs require: Literacy, education, and training, 1940–2006* [Policy information report, research division]. Princeton, NJ: Educational Testing Service.

Benesch, S. (1991). *ESL in America: Myths and possibilities.* Portsmouth, NH: Boynton/Cook.

BEST. (1984). *Basic English skills test manual, Form C*. Washington, D.C.: Center for Applied Linguistics.

Bliss, W.B. (1990). Meeting the demand for ESL instruction: A response to demographics. In F.P. Chisman and associates (Eds.), *Leadership for literacy* (pp. 171–197). San Francisco, CA: Jossey-Bass.

Border Summit on Adult Bilingual Education. (1998). Testimonies distributed at Border Summit, 20 October, El Paso, TX.

Brooke, B. (2000). Strength in numbers, *Hispanic* (January/February) 36–40.

Brown, B.L. (1998). *Applying constructivism in vocational and career education* [information series no. 378]. Columbus, OH: ERIC Clearinghouse on Adult, Career, and Vocational Education.

Brown, H.D. (1994). *Teaching by principles: An interactive approach to language pedagogy*. Englewood Cliffs, NJ: Prentice-Hall Regents.

Bureau of Labor Statistics. (1996). Worker Displacement during the mid 1990's. [Online]. Available: http://www.bls.census.gov/cps/pub/disp_0296.htm [1999, November 18].

Bureau of Labor Statistics. (2000). Labor force statistics from the current population survey: Displaced workers summary. [Online]. Available: http://stats.bls.gov/news.release.disp [2000, December 12].

Burt, M. and F. Keenan. (1998). Trends in staff development for adult ESL instructors [ERIC Q & A]. Washington, D.C.: National Clearinghouse for ESL Literacy Education.

CAL Reporter. (2000). BEST evolves to meet new needs. *CAL Reporter: Newsletter from the Center for Applied Linguistics* 14, 1–5.

Calderon, M. (1999). Survey of displaced workers' views about their ESL classes [unpublished manuscript submitted to the Texas Workforce Commission]. El Paso, TX: El Paso Adult Bilingual Curriculum Institute.

Cañas, J. (2000). Maquiladora's impact on El Paso and Juarez. Paper presented at a national conference, NAFTA Impact on the Border: Problems and Solutions, at the University of Texas, 5–6 October, El Paso, TX.

Carnevale, A. and K. Reich. (2000). *A piece of the puzzle: How states can use education to make work pay for welfare recipients*. Princeton, NJ: Educational Testing Service.

CASAS. (1997). Extending the ladder: From CASAS to work keys assessments [executive summary report]. San Diego, CA: Author.

CASAS. (2001). *Resource Catalog*. San Diego, CA: Author.

Center for Defense Information. (1999). Weekly defense monitor, 3 (9), 4–5. [Online]. Available: http://www.cdi.org/weekly/1999/issue09.html [2000, November 19].

Center on Budget and Policy Priorities. (2000). Windows of opportunity: Strategies to support low income families in the next stage of welfare reform. [Online]. Available: http://www.cbpp.org/3-30-00wel.pdf [2000, November 10].

Chapa, J. and C. Wacker. (2000). Latino unemployment: Current issues and future concerns. In S. Perez (Ed.), *Moving up the economic ladder: Latino workers and the nation's future prosperity* (pp. 61–87). Washington, D.C.: National Council of La Raza.

Chisman, F.P. (1990). Toward a literate America: The leadership challenge. In F.P. Chisman and associates (Eds.), *Leadership for literacy* (pp. 1–24). San Francisco, CA: Jossey-Bass.

Chisman, F.P. and W.L. Campbell. (1990). Narrowing the job-skills gap: A focus on workforce literacy. In F.P. Chisman and associates (Eds.), *Leadership for literacy* (pp. 144–170). San Francisco, CA: Jossey-Bass.

Colette, M., B. Woliver, M.B. Bingman, and J. Merrifield. (1996). *Getting there: A curriculum for moving people into employment.* Knoxville, TN: Center for Literacy Studies, University of Tennessee.

Collier, V.P. (1992). A synthesis of studies examining long-term language minority student data on academic achievement. *Bilingual Research Journal* 16 (1 & 2), 187–212.

Comings, J. (1999). Sick and tired of accountability. *The Change Agent* [newsletter of the New England Resource Center], 9, 8.

Cranton, P. (1997). *Transformative learning in action: Insights for practice* [New Directions for Continuing Education Series]. San Francisco, CA: Jossey- Bass.

Crawford, J. (1991). *Bilingual education: History, politics, theory and practice.* Los Angeles, CA: Bilingual Education Services.

CTB/McGraw-Hill. (2001). *Adult Assessment Products.* Monterey, CA: author.

Cummins, J. (1989). *Empowering minority students.* Sacramento, CA: California Association for Bilingual Education.

D'Amico, D. (1997). *Adult education and welfare to work initiatives: A review of research, practice, and policy* [Literacy Leader Fellowship Program Reports]. Washington, D.C.: National Institute for Literacy.

D'Amico, D. (1999). *Politics, policy, practice, and personal responsibility: Adult education in an era of welfare reform.* [NCSALL Report #10A]. Boston, MA: National Center for the Study of Adult Literacy.

D'Amico, D. and E. Schnee. (1997). "It Changed Something Inside Of Me: English Language Learning, Structural Barriers to Employment, and Workers' Goals in a Workplace Literacy Program." In G. Hull (Ed.), *Changing work, changing workers: Critical perspectives on language, literacy, and skills* (pp.117–140). Albany: State University of New York Press.

Daley, Barbara J. (2000). Learning in professional practice. In V.W. Mott and B.J. Daley (Eds.), *Charting a course for continuing professional education: Reframing professional practice* [Adult and Continuing Education series], (pp. 33–42). San Francisco, CA: Jossey-Bass.

Darrah, C. (1997). Complicating the concept of skill requirements: Scenes from a workplace. In G. Hull (Ed.), *Changing work, changing workers: Critical perspectives on language, literacy, and skills* (pp. 249–272). Albany: State University of New York Press.

Del Vecchio, A., C. Gustke, and J. Wilde. (1998). Alternative assessment for Latino students. In M. González, A. Huerta-Macías, and J. Tinajero (Eds.), *Educating Latino students: A guide to successful practice* (pp. 329–356). Lancaster, PA: Technomic.

Doane, T. (1998). Democracy and the ESL classroom. In T. Smoke (Ed.), *Adult ESL: Politics, pedagogy, and participation in classroom and community programs* (pp. 171–184). Mahwah, NJ: Lawrence Erlbaum Associates.

Donato, R. (1999). Hispano education and the implications of autonomy: Four school systems in southern Colorado, 1920–1963, *Harvard Educational Review* 69, 117–149.

Duffy, M. (2001). *La Frontera: A day at the border—A town hall meeting*. El Paso, TX: Presented by *Time*, CNN, AOL Latin America, and the University of Texas at El Paso, June 5.

El Paso Adult Bilingual Curriculum Institute. (2000). *Project summary*. El Paso, TX: author.

Faltis, C.J. and S.J. Hudelson. (1998). *Bilingual education in elementary and secondary school communities: Toward understanding and caring*. Needham Heights, MA: Allyn & Bacon.

Fisher, J.C. (1999). Research on adult literacy education in the welfare-to-work transition. In L.G. Martin and J.C. Fisher (Eds.), *The welfare-to-work challenge for adult literacy educator* 83, 29–42.

Flynn, K. (1997a). Advocates seek English training solution. *El Paso Times* (21 December).

Flynn, K. (1997b). Available high school jobs require English proficiency. *El Paso Times* (21 December).

Foster, S. (1990). Upgrading the skills of literacy professionals: The profession matures. In F.P. Chisman and associates (Eds.), *Leadership for literacy* (pp. 73–95). San Francisco, CA: Jossey-Bass.

Freeman, Y. and D. Freeman. (1998). *ESL/EFL teaching: Principles for success*. Portsmouth, NH: Heineman.

Freire, P. (1985). *The politics of education: culture, power, and liberation*. Granby, MA: Begin and Garvey.

Freire, P. (1998). *Teachers as cultural workers: Letters to those who dare teach*. Boulder, CO: Westview Press.

García, E.E. (1990). Instructional discourse in 'effective' Hispanic classrooms. In R. Jacobson and C. Faltis (Eds.), *Language distribution issues in bilingual schooling* (pp. 104–117). Bristol, PA: Multilingual Matters Ltd.

García, G.E. and P.D. Pearson. (1994). Assessment and diversity. In L. Darling-Hammond (Ed.), *Review of research in education* (pp. 337–392). Washington, D.C.: American Educational Research Association.

Garner, B. (1999). Nationwide accountability: The national reporting system, *Focus on Basics* 3, 11–12.

Gibbs, N. (2001). The new frontier: A whole new world, *TIME Special Issue* (21 December), 36–45.

Gillespie, M.K. (1996). *Learning to work in a new land: A review and sourcebook for vocational and workplace ESL*. Washington, D.C.: Center for Applied Linguistics.

González, M.L., A. Huerta-Macías, and J. Tinajero. (1998). *Educating Latinos: A guide to quality practice*. Lancaster, PA: Technomics.

Graman, T. (1988). Education for humanization: Applying Paolo Freire's pedagogy to learning a second language. *Harvard Educational Review* 58, 433–448.

Grognet, A.G. (1997). ERIC Q&A: Integrating employment skills in adult ESL instruction. Washington, D.C.: National Clearinghouse for ESL Literacy

Education. [Online]. Available: http://www.cal.org/ncle/digests/ EskillsQA.htm [2000, October 17].

Grubb, W.N. (1996). *Working in the middle: Strengthening education and training for the mid-skilled labor force.* San Francisco, CA: Jossey-Bass.

Guzmán, L.E. (2000). Written testimony presented at national conference, NAFTA Impact on the Border: Problems and Solutions, at The University of Texas, 5–6 October, El Paso, TX.

Hart-Landsberg, S. and S. Reder, S. (1997). Teamwork and liteacy: Teaching and learning at Hardy Industries. In G. Hull (Ed.), *Changing work, changing workers: Critical perspectives on language, literacy, and skills* (pp. 350–382). Albany: State University of New York Press.

Hayes, C.W., R. Bahruth, and C. Kessler. (1991). *Literacy con cariño.* Portsmouth, NH: Heinemann Educational Books.

Hayes, E. (1999). Policy issues that drive the transformation of adult literacy. *The Welfare-to-Work Challenge for Adult Literacy Educators* [New Directions for Adult and Continuing Education Series] 83, 3–14.

Heath, S.B. (1989). Sociocultural contexts of language development. In *Beyond language: Social and cultural factors in schooling language minority students* (pp. 148–186). Los Angeles, CA: Bilingual Education Office, State Department of Education.

Heyck, D. (1994). *Barrios and borderlands: Cultures of Latinos and Latinas in the United States.* New York, NY: Routledge.

Houde, A.P. (2000a). Anamarc Educational Institute [Program brochure]. El Paso, TX: Author.

Houde, A.P. (2000b). What's working in our institution and what we need. Paper presented at national conference, NAFTA Impact on the Border: Problems and Solutions, at the University of Texas, 5–6 October, El Paso, TX.

Huerta, A. (1978). Code-switching among Spanish-English bilinguals: A sociolinguistic perspective. Ph.D. diss., University of Texas, Austin.

Huerta-Macías, A. (In press). Getting an even start: A story of family literacy through participation and collaboration. Washington, D.C.: TESOL Publications.

Hull, G. (1993). "Hearing Other Voices: A Critical Assessment of Popular Voices on Literacy and Work." *Harvard Educational Review* 63(1), 20–49.

Imel, S. (1999). Work force education: Beyond technical skills [Trends and Issues Alert No. 1]. Columbus, OH: ERIC Clearinghouse on Adult, Career, and Vocational Education.

Jacobson, R. (1990). Allocating two languages as a key feature of a bilingual methodology. In R. Jacobson and C. Faltis (Eds.), *Language distribution issues in bilingual schooling* (pp. 3–17). Bristol, PA: Multilingual Matters Ltd.

Jenkins, D. (1999). *Beyond welfare-to-work: Bridging the low-wage-livable-wage employment gap.* Chicago, IL: Great Cities Institute, University of Illinois at Chicago.

Jobs for the Future. (1999). Work-related learning guide for family literacy and adult education organizations. Boston, MA: Author.

Keating, G. (1996). *Superstudy II.* New York, NY: McGraw-Hill.

Knell, S. (1998). *Learn to earn: Issues raised by welfare reform for adult education.* Washington, D.C.: National Institute for Literacy. [Online]. Available: http://www.nifl.gov/activities/sknell.htm [2000, September 30].

Kolenc, V. (1998). Job retraining focuses on employer buy-in. *El Paso Times* (9 August), E1.

Kolenc, V. (2000). Job retraining project awaits extension. *El Paso Times* (25 June), E1.

Kramer, W. 1995. The Politics of Production: Post-Fordist Popular Sector Substitutions and Strategies. Unpublished manuscript submitted for an independent study.

Krashen, S.D. (1996). *Under attack: The case against bilingual education.* Culver City, CA: Language Education Associates.

Kutner, M. (1992). *ERIC Digest: Staff development for ABE and ESL teachers and volunteers.* Washington, D.C., National Clearinghouse on Literacy Education.

Labor Market Information. 1997. [Online]. Available: http://www.twc.state.tx.us/svcs/taa/qa1–4.html [1999, December 16].

Lankard, B.A. (1995). SCANS and the new vocationalism. [ERIC Digest]. ERIC Clearinghouse on Adult, Career, and Vocational Education. Columbus, OH: Center on Education and Training for Employment at Ohio State University.

Larmer, B. (1999). Latino America, *Newsweek* (12 July) 48–64.

Lee, C. (1995). Out of the maze: Can the federal job-training mess be fixed? *Training* (February) 29–36.

Lobb, N. (1997). *16 extraordinary Hispanic Americans.* Portland, ME: J. Weston Walch.

Lockwood, A.T. (1996). *Caring, community, and personalization: Strategies to combat the Hispanic dropout problem.* Washington, D.C.: U.S. Department of Education/Hispanic Dropout Project.

Lucas, T. (1997). *Into, through, and beyond secondary school: Critical transitions for immigrant youths.* McHenry, IL: Center for Applied Linguistics and Delta Systems.

Macías, R.F. (1994). Inheriting sins while seeking absolution: Language diversity and national data sets. In D. Spener (Ed.), *Adult biliteracy in the United States* (pp. 15–46). McHenry, IL: Center for Applied Linguistics and Delta Systems.

McAlmon, G. (1999). Workers Don't Find NAFTA So Appealing. *El Paso Times* (14 November), 13A.

McGroarty, M. and S. Scott. (1993). Workplace ESL instruction: Varieties and constraints [ERIC Digest]. [Online]. Available: http://www.cal.org/ncle/digests/WORKPLACE_ESL.HTML [2000, October 17].

McKay, S.L. (1993). *Agendas for second language literacy.* New York, NY: Cambridge University Press.

Melendez, E. (1996). *Working on jobs: The center for employment training.* Boston, MA: The Mauricio Gastón Institute.

Merriam, S.B. and R.S. Caffarella. (1999). *Learning in adulthood: A comprehensive guide.* San Francisco, CA: Jossey-Bass.

Merrifield, J. (1997). If job training is the answer, what is the question? Research with displaced women textile workers. In G. Hull (Ed.), *Changing work, changing workers: Critical perspectives on language, literacy, and skills* (pp. 273–294). Albany: State University of New York Press.

Merrifield, J. (1998). *Contested ground: Performance accountability in adult basic education* [NCSALL Research Brief]. Boston, MA: National Center for the Study of Adult Learning and Literacy.

Merrifield, J. (1999). Performance accountability: For what? To whom? and how? *Focus on Basics* 3, 6–10.

MET, Inc. (nd) Motivation Education & Training [program brochure]. One-Stop Career Service Center; El Paso, TX: MET, Inc.

MET, Inc. (2000). Information flyers for applicants. El Paso, TX: Author.

Mezirow, J. (1991). *Transformative dimensions of adult learning*. San Francisco, CA: Jossey-Bass.

Morales, R. (2000). What a Latino finds in the U.S. labor market. In S. Perez (Ed.), *Moving up the economic ladder: Latino workers and the nation's future prosperity* (pp. 35–60). Washington, D.C.: National Council of La Raza.

Moreno, J. (1997). Border city struggles to mend loss of apparel industry: El Paso's torn fabric. *Houston Chronicle* (12 December).

Murnane, R.J., J.B. Willett, and J.H. Tyler. (2000). Who benefits from obtaining a GED? Evidence from high school and beyond [NCSALL Research Briefs]. Boston, MA: National Center for the Study of Adult Learning and Literacy.

Myerson, A.R. (1997). Low wage workers have been losing jobs to Mexico. *New York Times*. (8 May) [Online]. Available: http://mtholyoke.edu/acad/intrel/naftjobs.htm

NAFTA impact on the border: Problems and solutions. (2000). National conference held at the University of Texas, 5–6 October, El Paso, TX.

National Center on Adult Literacy. (1995). Adult Literacy: The next generation. [paper prepared for Literacy Policy Forum, 17 March 1995, Library of Congress]. Philadelphia, PA: author.

National Center for Education Statistics. (1996). 1992 National adult literacy survey. [Online]. Available: http://www.nces.gov/pubs2000/surveys:NADLITS.overview [2000, June 5].

National Center for Education Statistics. (1998). Adult participation in English as a second language (ESL) classes [NCES 98–036]. Retrieved on October 25, 2000 from the world wide web: http://nces.ed.gov/pubs98/98036.html.

National Center for Education Statistics. (1999a). Digest of education statistics. [Online]. Available: http://nces.ed.gov/pubs2000/Digest99/d99t363.html [2000, October 18].

National Center for Education Statistics. (1999b). Digest of education statistics. [Online]. Available: http://nces.ed.gov/pubs2000/Digest99/d99t389.html [2000, October 18].

National Center for Health Statistics. (2000). *Race and ethnicity: Fertility rates.* [Online]. Available: http://www.ameristat.org/racethnic/fertility.htm [2000, November 7].

National Council of Latino Executives. (1999). Advocating for Latinos in child welfare. [Published by Child Welfare League of America]. [Online]. Available: http://www.cwla.org/latexecs/councillatinoexecs.html [2000, November 7].

National Institute for Literacy (2000a). Fact sheet: English for speakers of other languages. [Online]. Available: http://www.nifl.gov/newworld/WEL-FARE.HTM [2000, September 18].

National Institute for Literacy. (2000b). Fact sheet: Welfare recipients generally have low education skills. [Online]. Available: http://www.nifl.gov/newworld/WELFARE.HTM [2000, September 26].

National Institute for Literacy. (2000c). *From the margins to the mainstream: An action agenda for literacy* [The National Literacy Summit 2000]. Washington, D.C.: Author.

National Institute for Literacy. (2000d). *Literacy skills for the twenty-first century: A blueprint for creating a more literate nation.* Washington, D.C.: Author.

National Reporting System for Adult Education. (2000). [Online]. Available: http://www.air-dc.org/nrs [2001, March 13].

National Research Council. (2000). *How people learn: Brain, mind, experience, and school.* Washington, D.C.: National Academy Press.

National Skills Standards Board Frequently Asked Questions. (2000). The NSSB: A brief description. [Online]. Available: www.nssb.org [2001, March 20].

New Mexico State Department of Education. (2001). *Adult basic education: Journeys of the heart* [annual report, 1999–2000]. Santa Fe, NM: Author.

Nightingale, D.S. and J. Trutko. (1999). Status of the welfare-to-work (WtW) grants program after one year. Washington, D.C.: Urban Institute. [Online]. Available: http://www.urban.org/welfare/wtw_labor.html [2000, November 2].

Oboler, S. (1995). *Ethnic labels, Latino lives: Latino identity and the politics of (re)presentation in the United States.* Minneapolis, MN: University of Minnesota Press.

Olsen, L. (1997). *Made in America: Immigrant students in our public schools.* New York, NY: The New Press.

Padgett, T. and Thomas, C.B. (2001). Two countries, one city, *TIME Special Issue* (11 June), 64–66.

Peace Action Education. (1999). Fact sheet: Hunger is growing in America. [Online]. Available: http://www.webcom.com/peaceact/hunger_v_military.html [2000, November 9].

Perez, S. (2000). *Moving up the economic ladder: Latino workers and the nation's prosperity.* Washington, D.C.: National Council of La Raza.

Pfaff, C. (1979). Constraints on language mixing: Intrasentential code-switching and borrowing in Spanish/English, *Language* 55, 291–318.

Poplack, S. (1980). Sometimes I'll start a sentence in Spanish y termino en Español: Towards a typology of code-switching, *Linguistics* 18, 581–618.

PREP Program Data. (2001). *Update on PREP* [one page information sheet] (15 July), El Paso, TX: Upper Rio Grande Workforce Development Board Quality Assurance.

Purcell-Gates, V., S. Degener, and E. Jacobson. (1998). *U.S. adult literacy program practice: A typology across dimensions of life-contextualized/decontextualized and dialogic/monologic* [NCSALL Brief]. Philadelphia, PA: National Center on Adult Literacy.

Quigley, B.A. (1997). *Rethinking literacy education: The critical need for practice-based change.* San Francisco, CA: Jossey-Bass.

Ramirez, J.D. (1992). Executive summary. *Bilingual Research Journal* 16 (1 & 2), 1–62.

Richard-Amato, P.A. (1996). *Making it happen: Interaction in the second language classroom.* White Plains, NY: Addison-Wesley.

Rivera, K. (1999a). *Native language literacy and adult ESL instruction* [ERIC Digest]. Washington, D.C.: Center for Applied Linguistics.

Rivera, K.M. (1999b). From developing one's voice to making oneself heard: Affecting language policy from the bottom up. In T. Huebner and K.A. Davis (Eds.), *Sociopolitical perspectives on language policy and planning in the USA* (pp. 333–346). Philadelphia, PA: John Benjamin Publishing Company.

Rodriguez, C. (2000). Legal remedies available to trade affected workers: Problems with access and enforcement. Paper presented at national conference, NAFTA Impact on the Border: Problems and Solutions, at the University of Texas, 5–6 October, El Paso, TX.

Rodriguez, E. and K. Kirk. (2000). *Welfare reform, TANF, caseload changes, and Latinos: A preliminary assessment* [NCLR Issue Brief No. 3]. Washington, D.C.: National Council of La Raza.

Rodriguez, R., N.J. Ramos, and J.A. Ruiz-Escalante. (1994). *Compendium of readings in bilingual education: Issues and practices.* San Antonio, TX: Texas Association for Bilingual Education.

Romo, H.D. and T. Falbo. (1996). *Latino high school graduation: Defying the odds.* Austin, TX: University of Texas Press.

Rosen, H. (2000). Paper presented at national conference, NAFTA Impact on the Border: Problems and Solutions, at the University of Texas, 5–6 October, El Paso, TX.

Rosenblum, S. (1996). Union-sponsored workplace ESL instruction [ERIC Digest]. [Online]. Available: http://www.cal.org/ncle/digests/ROSENBLU. HTM [2000, October 17].

Santos, R. and P. Seitz. (2000). Benefit coverage for Latino and Latina workers. In S. Pérez (Ed.), *Moving up the economic ladder: Latino workers and the nation's future prosperity* (pp. 162–185). Washington, D.C.: National Council of La Raza.

Schultz, K. (1992). *Training for basic skills or educating workers? Changing conceptions of workplace education programs.* Berkeley, CA: National Center for Research in Vocational Education at the University of California.

Shanahan, T., M. Meehan, and S. Mogge. (1995). *The professionalization of the adult literacy teacher* [NCAL Brief]. Philadelphia, PA: National Center on Adult Literacy.

Sharp, J. 1998. *Bordering the Future: Challenge and Opportunity in the Texas Border Region.* Austin, TX: Texas Comptroller's Office.

Siles, M. and S.M. Perez. (2000). What Latino workers bring to the labor market: How human capital affects employment outcomes. In S. Perez (Ed.), *Moving up the economic ladder: Latino workers and the nation's future prosperity* (pp. 1–34). Washington, D.C.: National Council of La Raza.

Silva-Corvalán, C. (1983). Code-shifting patterns in Chicano Spanish. In L. Elias-Olivares (Ed.), *Spanish in the U.S. setting: Beyond the southwest* (pp. 69–88). Wheaton, MD: National Clearinghouse for Bilingual Education.

Smoke, T. (1998). *Adult ESL: Politics, pedagogy, and participation in classroom and community programs.* Mahwah, NJ: Lawrence Erlbaum Associates.

Soifer, R., M.E. Irwin, B. Crumrine, E. Honzaki, B. Simmons, D. Young. (1990). *The complete theory-to-practice handbook of adult literacy: Curriculum design and teaching approaches.* New York, NY: Teachers College press.

Sparks, B. (1999). Critical issues and dilemmas for adult literacy programs under welfare reform. In L.G. Martin and J.C. Fisher (Eds.), *The welfare-to-work challenge for adult literacy educators* 83, 15–28.

Spener, D. (1993). The Freirian approach to adult literacy education. In J. Crandall and J. Peyton (Eds.), *Approaches to adult ESL literacy instruction* (pp. 75–98). Washington, D.C.: Center for Applied Linguistics and Delta Systems Company.

Stein, S.G. (1997). *Equipped for the future: A reform agenda for adult literacy and lifelong learning.* Washington, D.C.: National Institute for Literacy.

Stein, S.G. (2000). *Equipped for the future content standards: What adults need to know and be able to do in the 21st* century. Washington, D.C.: National Institute for Literacy.

Templan, N. (2000). Anatomy of a job program that went awry. *Wall Street Journal* (11 February), 1B.

TESOL Task Force. (2000). *Program standards for adult education ESOL programs.* Arlington, VA: TESOL.

Texas Border Infrastructure Coalition. (2000). *Workforce development and education report.* Laredo, TX: Author.

Texas Education Agency. (n.d.) *Texas adult education annual performance report: Fiscal year 1992–1993.* Austin, TX: Author.

Texas Workforce Commission. (nd) Total Quality Workforce Literacy for Texas: Indicators of Program Quality. Austin, TX: Author.

Tim, L.A. (1993). Bilingual code-switching: An overview of research. In B.J. Merino, H. Trueba, and F. Samaniego (Eds.), *Language and culture in learning: Teaching Spanish to native speakers of Spanish* (pp. 94–112). Bristol, PA: Falmer Press.

Tondre-El Zorkani, B. (2001). Literacy and language services for Texas' Spanish-speaking dislocated workers: The devil is in the details. Austin, TX: A Research report for the Texas Workforce Commission.

Torres-Guzmán, M., C.I. Mercade, A.H. Quintero, and D.R. Viera. (1994). Teaching and learning in Puerto-Rican/Latino collaboratives: Implications for teacher education. In E.R. Hollins, J.E. King, and W.C. Hayman (Eds.), *Teaching diverse populations: Formulating a knowledge base* (pp. 105–129). Albany, NY: New York Press.

Trueba, H. (1990). The role of culture in literacy acquisition: An interdisciplinary approach to qualitative research, *International Journal of Qualitative Studies in Education,* 3 (1), 1–13.

U.S. Census Bureau. (2001). *The Hispanic population: Census 2000 brief.* Washington, D.C.: U.S. Department of Commerce.

U.S. Department of Education. (1998). Workplace literacy. [Online]. Available: http://www.ed.gov/offices/OVAE/AdultEd/InfoBoard/f-16.html.

U.S. Department of Education. (2000a). *National education goals*. [Online]. Available: http://www.ed.gov/legislation/GOALS2000/TheAct/sec102.html [2000, October 17].

U.S. Department of Education. (2000b). *FY2001 Budget Summary*. Retrieved on November 9, 2000 from the world wide web: http://www.ed.gov/offices/OUS/Budget01/BudgetSumm/sum-d.html.

U.S. Department of Labor. (1995). The one-stop career center system. [Online]. Available: http://www.doleta.gov/progams/factsht/one-stop.htm.

U.S. Department of Labor. (2000). Job training partnership act. [Online]. Available: http://www.doleta.gov/programs/factsht/jtpa.asp [2000, October 17].

Valdés, G. (1996). *Con respeto: Bridging the distances between culturally diverse families and schools, an ethnographic portrait*. New York, NY: Teachers College Press.

Van Duzer, C.H. & R. Berdan. (2000). Perspectives on assessment in adult ESOL instruction. In J. Comings, B. Garner, and C. Smith (Eds.), *Annual review of adult learning and literacy* 1, 200–242. San Francisco, CA: Jossey-Bass.

Verdecia, C. (2001). Census and sensibility. *Hispanic Magazine* (April), 8.

Waggoner, D. (1997). Study documents demand for adult ESL classes. *TESOL Matters* (October/November), 14.

Weil, A. (2000). *Where is welfare reform heading?* [Online]. Available: http://www.urban.org/news/press/weil09–22–00.htm [2000, November 6].

Weinstein-Shr, G. and E. Quintero. (1995). *Immigrant learners and their families*. McHenry, IL: Center for Applied Linguistics and Delta Systems.

White House Initiative on Educational Excellence for Hispanic Americans. (1999). *Latinos in education*. Washington, D.C.: U.S. Department of Education.

Wilson, A.L. (2000). Professional practice in the modern world. In V.W. Mott and B.J. Daley (Eds.), *Charting a course for continuing professional education: Reframing professional practice* [Adult and Continuing Education series], (pp. 71–79). San Francisco, CA: Jossey-Bass.

Woodcock, R.W. (1991). *Woodcock Language Proficiency Battery—Revised*. Itasca, IL: Riverside.

Woodcock, R.W. and A.F. Muñoz-Sandoval. (1995). *Woodcock-Language Proficiency Battery—Revised, Spanish*. Itasca, IL: Riverside.

Wrigley, H. (2001). Assessment and accountability: A modest proposal. *Field notes newsletter* 10(3), 1–7. [Online]. Available: www.sabes.org [2001, March 22].

Wrigley, H.S., F. Chisman, and D. Ewen. (1993). *Sparks of excellence: Program realities and promising practices in adult ESL*. Washington, D.C.: Southport Institute for Policy Analysis.

Index

About the Author

ANA G. HUERTA-MACÍAS is Associate Professor, Department of Curriculum and Instruction, New Mexico State University.